LOW-CARB
COOKING
with Your INSTANT POT®

LOW-CARB COOKING

with Your **INSTANT POT**®

80 Fast & Easy Family Meals

EMILY SUNWELL-VIDAURRI **&** RUDY VIDAURRI

Coauthors of *Amazing Mexican Favorites with Your Instant Pot*® and creators of Recipes to Nourish

PAGE STREET
PUBLISHING CO.

PAGE STREET
PUBLISHING CO.

Copyright © 2019 Rodolfo Vidaurri and Emily Sunwell-Vidaurri

First published in 2019 by
Page Street Publishing Co.
27 Congress Street, Suite 105
Salem, MA 01970
www.pagestreetpublishing.com

Distributed by Macmillan, sales in Canada by The Canadian Manda Group.

23 22 21 20 19   1 2 3 4 5

ISBN-13: 978-1-62414-790-6
ISBN-10: 1-62414-790-9

Library of Congress Control Number: 2018964666

Cover and book design by Laura Gallant for Page Street Publishing Co.
Photography by Emily Sunwell-Vidaurri

Printed and bound in China

Instant Pot® is a registered trademark of Double Insight, Inc., which was not involved in the creation of this book.

FOR LITTLE LOVE, TINY LOVE AND OUR TWINKLES.

Dedicated to all the readers being mindful of taking care of their health by choosing to eat home-cooked, from-scratch, real food.

CONTENTS

INTRODUCTION

The idea of having your cake and eating it too is not as far-fetched as it seems with *Low-Carb Cooking with Your Instant Pot®*. With the recipes in this book, you can indulge in abundance and flavor—two things not usually associated with low-carb meals—without any guilt.

The unique challenge of writing a low-carb cookbook is to translate wholesome, classic, flavor-packed recipes into a tight bundle of healthy alternatives that produce the same satisfaction you would get from eating carb-packed food. It is our joy to introduce these low-carb meals that we eat as a family.

We also take great pride in making these recipes accessible to people with dietary restrictions or who simply want to eat a diet lower in carbs. Combine this with the fact that the Instant Pot delivers these meals in a fraction of the time it would take to cook them the old-fashioned way, and you have a recipe for success.

Often, people find that they simply don't have the time to prepare healthy, home-cooked meals. They find themselves stuck in a rut, eating fast food or takeout while their health suffers. This is where the incredibly helpful kitchen tool, the Instant Pot, comes into play.

This cookbook is designed to help ensure a quick and timely prep process and fast cooking time so that homemade meals won't be so much of a chore. Using the Instant Pot means that you do not have to take on a load of several pots and pans to wash by the time you're done cooking your meal. You don't even have to stress about eating healthy on road-trip vacations anymore because the Instant Pot travels with you—all you need is an electrical outlet.

While this cookbook's main focus is low-carb food, it's important to note that everyone's health needs are different. There are small amounts of carrots, onions and celeriac (a.k.a. celery root) used in some of the recipes. If you know that your diet requires very careful monitoring of carbs, you might need to consider making substitutions when these ingredients are used.

For example, "aboveground" vegetables such as spinach, lettuce, cauliflower, zucchini, eggplant, asparagus, green beans and so on tend to be lower in carbs than "belowground" veggies like carrots, onions, celeriac, parsnips, beets and the like. The same rule of thumb doesn't necessarily apply to fruits, so it's best to make sure you know what is safe or right for your body. Usually, the best fruits to choose for low-carb eating are berries, tomatoes, olives, citrus, plums and peaches—and that's what you'll find in this cookbook.

When it comes to the ingredients in this cookbook, we focus on real food. You will not find processed foods or imitation foods—just plain and simple, real-food ingredients. This cookbook reflects the cooking style from my blog and the way my family eats. This means whole, organic, real food. All the recipes in this cookbook are gluten-free, grain-free and low-carb.

While not specifically listed in the ingredients (except for grass-fed butter), my hope is that you'll choose to use meats, dairy, eggs and healthy fats that come from grass-fed or pasture-raised animals. "Grass-fed" and "pasture-raised" imply that the animal was fed a species-appropriate diet, which in turn means it is healthier for you and your body. My intention with the ingredients in this book is that they are meant to nourish your body, not pollute it with processed foods, pesticides and chemicals.

While not every ingredient in the book says "organic," we recommend shopping from the yearly updated Environmental Working Group's lists of produce called the Dirty Dozen™ and Clean Fifteen™. These list the fruits and vegetables that are the most contaminated with pesticides and chemicals and the ones that are the safest to consume.

When it comes down to it, we're all trying to do the best we can when it comes to our health. Most likely, if you're choosing to eat low-carb, you're doing so because you're working on your health or wanting to make some changes in your dietary lifestyle.

While for some people eating healthy, nourishing meals made from whole foods is a trend, for us it is a lifestyle. As a real-food, gluten-free blogger and three-time cookbook author, it is my responsibility to practice what I preach—and my main mission is to help support my readers' wellness. I started my blog in 2011 to help show others that natural living and eating healthy, real food doesn't have to be complicated. Since I started my blog, health trends have changed a lot, and more and more people are becoming aware of and in tune with their bodies and seeking dietary lifestyles beyond gluten-free and Paleo like ketogenic, Autoimmune Protocol, GAPS and low-carb. Because we are all so different and we believe that there is not one "perfect" diet that fits all, we wanted to give our readers low-carb choices that are just as nourishing, delectable and satisfying as the heavier-carb alternatives, regardless of your dietary lifestyle.

Rudy's path as an athlete, mixed martial artist and trainer geared his approach to nutrition as a science to fine-tune his body. Throughout his years as a nationally-ranked swimmer, he was always looking for a natural edge in performance. Now he applies the same philosophy to his preparation for competitions in the arena of mixed martial arts. His daily training regimen is extremely rigorous and maintaining a balanced, healthy diet is critical to optimal performance. Rudy's additional experience as a seasoned chef has helped him translate the necessary dietary requirements it takes to perform at a high level. By honing his craft as a cook, he's been able to develop recipes that can be applicable to any person's nutritional needs. It is his great pride as a two-time cookbook author to help people from all walks of life eat their very best.

We believe that everyone can benefit from eating real food—fresh, whole, nutrient-dense, non-GMO, unprocessed food—and that is our goal here, with a low-carb spin!

We hope that this cookbook brings you some relief when it comes to low-carb meal planning and that you enjoy these simple and delicious recipes as much as we do.

Emily Sunwell-Vidaurri   Rudy Vidaurri

COMFORT FOODS WITHOUT THE CARBS

Classic comfort foods can warm your soul, make you feel cozy, take you back to a special time in your life or simply envelop you with that feeling of a big loving hug. The Instant Pot reinvents all of your favorites in a quick and convenient way at the press of a button.

With these low-carb versions of comforting, nostalgic recipes, you can still enjoy the pure yumminess without the heaviness of grains and starchy foods. Even better, these recipes are so delicious, you won't miss the carbs at all!

Take a trip down your culinary memory lane with low-carb dishes like Spicy Buffalo Chicken Wings (page 25) and Low-Carb Green Bean Casserole (page 29).

LOW-CARB SWEET AND SOUR CHICKEN

PREP TIME: 25 MINUTES
COOK TIME: 20 MINUTES
TOTAL TIME: 45 MINUTES
YIELD: 3 TO 4 SERVINGS

This classic Chinese takeout entrée is one of those comfort foods that has become highly popular and beloved all over the world. Typically, the protein in this dish is breaded and deep-fried, but this deeply flavored, low-carb version is equally delicious.

2 tbsp (30 g) grass-fed butter or ghee

3–4 (4-oz [112-g]) boneless and skinless chicken thighs, cut into 2-inch (5-cm) cubes

3 cloves garlic, finely chopped

¾-inch (19-mm) piece fresh ginger, peeled and minced or grated

2 scallions (white and light green parts only), thinly sliced, plus more as needed

2 tbsp (10 g) fresh lemongrass, finely chopped

2 tbsp (30 ml) apple cider vinegar

Zest of 1 orange

¼ cup (60 ml) freshly squeezed orange juice

1 tbsp (15 ml) coconut aminos or liquid aminos

2 tbsp (32 g) tomato paste

1 tsp sea salt

⅓ cup (67 g) granulated erythritol

1 medium red or orange bell pepper, top and seeds removed, cut into 2-inch (5-cm) pieces

1 medium green bell pepper, top and seeds removed, cut into 2-inch (5-cm) pieces

1 tbsp (3 g) fresh Thai basil or sweet basil, thinly sliced (optional)

Add the butter to the Instant Pot and press Sauté. Once the butter has melted, add the chicken, stirring occasionally until the chicken is browned on most sides, 7 minutes. Add the garlic, ginger, scallions and lemongrass and sauté for 2 minutes until fragrant, stirring occasionally. Add the vinegar, orange zest, orange juice, coconut aminos, tomato paste, salt and erythritol, stirring until the tomato paste has dissolved and is incorporated. Press Keep Warm/Cancel.

Add the bell peppers and basil to the Instant Pot, gently stirring until mostly incorporated.

Place the lid on the Instant Pot, making sure the steam-release valve is sealed. Press the Manual button and set for 6 minutes.

When the Instant Pot beeps, press Keep Warm/Cancel. Allow the Instant Pot to release its pressure naturally for 10 minutes. Using an oven mitt, open the steam-release valve. If there is any steam left over, allow it to release until the silver dial drops, then carefully open the lid.

Press Sauté and allow the sauce to come to a boil, then simmer for 5 minutes to allow the sauce to thicken. Press Keep Warm/Cancel and allow the sweet and sour chicken to rest for 10 minutes before serving (the sauce will thicken more as it rests).

Serve the sweet and sour chicken immediately, garnished with additional scallions. If you'd like a low-carb version of the traditional takeout-with-rice experience, this dish is delicious served with sautéed riced cauliflower instead of white rice.

NOTE: Erythritol is used as a low-carb sweetener in this recipe in place of traditional white sugar (used in most restaurants) or a natural sweetener like honey. This granulated low-carb sweetener is easy to find in natural-foods stores and is readily available online.

HEALTHY PESTO CHICKEN ALFREDO

PREP TIME: 25 MINUTES
COOK TIME: 17 MINUTES
TOTAL TIME: 42 MINUTES
YIELD: 3 TO 4 SERVINGS

Alfredo sauce with a hint of lemon, garlic and basil is one of our favorites! This creamy sauce goes perfectly with hearty bites of chicken. There's even a nice serving of veggies mixed into this rich and delectable dish.

3 tbsp (45 g) grass-fed butter or ghee

3 (4-oz [112-g]) boneless and skinless chicken breasts, cut into 1½-inch (4-cm) cubes

4 cloves garlic, finely chopped

¼ cup (60 ml) chicken broth

1 cup (240 ml) heavy cream

1 cup (240 g) cream cheese, softened

1 tsp sea salt

1 small head cauliflower, cut into bite-size florets

Zest of 1 lemon

1 cup (24 g) fresh basil, thinly sliced, plus more as needed

¼ cup (15 g) finely chopped fresh Italian parsley

¾ cup (75 g) grated Parmesan cheese

Add the butter to the Instant Pot and press Sauté. Once the butter has melted, add the chicken and stir occasionally until the chicken is browned on most sides, 7 minutes. Add the garlic and sauté for 2 minutes, stirring occasionally. Press Keep Warm/Cancel.

Add the chicken broth, cream, cream cheese and salt to the Instant Pot, stirring until mostly incorporated. Add the cauliflower and stir to combine.

Place the lid on the Instant Pot, making sure the steam-release valve is sealed. Press the Manual button and set for 8 minutes.

When the Instant Pot beeps, press Keep Warm/Cancel. Allow the Instant Pot to release its pressure naturally for 15 minutes. Using an oven mitt, open the steam-release valve. If there is any steam left over, allow it to release until the silver dial drops, then carefully open the lid.

Add the lemon zest, basil, parsley and Parmesan cheese to the Instant Pot, stirring until the Parmesan is fully incorporated.

Serve immediately, garnished with additional basil.

CHEESY VEGGIE-STUFFED MEATLOAF

PREP TIME: 25 MINUTES
COOK TIME: 32 MINUTES
TOTAL TIME: 57 MINUTES
YIELD: 4 TO 6 SERVINGS

This homestyle, breadcrumb-free comfort food is jam-packed with veggies, healthy fats and three cheeses. It's extra special served with Low-Carb Turnip and Celery Root Mash (page 133) and Garlic-Herb Brussels Sprouts (page 138). It cooks in less than half of the time it would take to bake a meatloaf too!

2 tbsp (30 g) grass-fed butter or ghee or 2 tbsp (30 ml) avocado oil

½ cup (38 g) coarsely chopped mushrooms

1 small zucchini, grated

1 small carrot, peeled and grated

1 large celery rib, diced

2 scallions (white parts only), finely chopped

5 oz (150 g) frozen chopped spinach, thawed and moisture squeezed out

1 lb (454 g) ground beef

1 large egg

1 tsp sea salt

1 tsp granulated garlic or garlic powder

1 tsp dried dill

1 tsp dried thyme

½ tsp onion powder

½ cup (30 g) finely chopped fresh Italian parsley

1 cup (120 g) shredded cheddar cheese

½ cup (56 g) shredded provolone or mozzarella cheese

½ cup (50 g) shredded Parmesan cheese

1 cup (240 ml) filtered water

Add the butter to the Instant Pot and press Sauté. Once the butter has melted, add the mushrooms, zucchini, carrot, celery, scallions and spinach and sauté for 7 minutes, stirring occasionally. Press Keep Warm/Cancel.

Using a slotted spoon, carefully transfer the cooked vegetables to a large piece of cheesecloth or a clean kitchen towel. Wrap the veggies up and tightly squeeze out any excess liquid. Set aside.

Place a large piece of foil on a flat surface. Place a large piece of parchment paper on top of the foil. Set aside.

In a large bowl, combine the ground beef, cooked and drained veggies, egg, salt, granulated garlic, dill, thyme, onion powder, parsley, cheddar cheese, provolone cheese and Parmesan cheese. Gently mix until everything is combined. Transfer the mixture to the parchment paper and form it into a meatloaf shape, being mindful of the size of your Instant Pot—the thickest part of the meatloaf should be no more than 3½ inches (9 cm) thick. Wrap the parchment paper–lined foil up around the meatloaf, leaving a small opening at the top.

Place the Instant Pot trivet inside the Instant Pot, then pour in the water and carefully place the meatloaf packet on top of the trivet. Place the lid on the Instant Pot, making sure the steam-release valve is sealed. Press the Manual button and set the Instant Pot for 25 minutes.

When the Instant Pot beeps, press Keep Warm/Cancel. Using an oven mitt, "quick release" the steam-release valve. When the steam stops venting and the silver dial drops, carefully open the lid. Using a meat thermometer, test the meatloaf to confirm that the internal temperature is at least 160°F (71°C) in the thickest part.

Carefully remove the meatloaf packet from the Instant Pot and gently unwrap the packet. Transfer the meatloaf to a serving plate and allow it to rest for 10 to 15 minutes before slicing, then serve immediately.

NOTE: If you prefer a sauce on top of your meatloaf, cook the meatloaf topped with ½ cup (120 ml) of low-carb ketchup or barbecue sauce.

SAUCY, SWEET AND TANGY BERRY PULLED PORK

PREP TIME: 25 MINUTES
COOK TIME: 56 MINUTES
TOTAL TIME: 81 MINUTES
YIELD: 6 TO 8 SERVINGS

Pulled pork is one of my husband's and little one's favorites—they easily devour second helpings. I'll be honest: Pork is not my preferred meat, so when we make it I need it to have lots of flavor, and sweet and tangy is always my favorite. This pulled pork is so delicious with the berries mixed into the herbed meat.

2 tbsp (30 g) grass-fed butter, ghee or 4 tbsp (60 ml) avocado oil

1 (2-to 3-lb [908- to 1.4-kg]) pork shoulder

4 cloves garlic, finely chopped

1 tsp fresh thyme leaves

½ tsp finely chopped fresh rosemary

¼ cup (60 ml) apple cider vinegar

¾ cup (180 ml) chicken broth

½ cup (120 ml) dry white wine

2 tbsp (25 g) granulated erythritol

1½ tsp (8 g) sea salt

1½ cups (233 g) fresh or frozen blueberries

½ cup (72 g) fresh or frozen blackberries

Add the butter to the Instant Pot and press Sauté. Once the butter has melted, add the pork roast and brown it for about 3½ minutes per side. Remove the roast and transfer it to a plate. Set it aside.

Add the garlic, thyme and rosemary to the Instant Pot and sauté for 2 minutes, until fragrant, stirring occasionally. Add the vinegar, broth, wine, erythritol and salt, stirring with a wooden spoon to scrape up any browned bits. Press Keep Warm/Cancel.

Place the browned roast in the Instant Pot and put on the lid, making sure the steam-release valve is sealed. Press the Manual button and set the Instant Pot for 35 minutes.

When the Instant Pot beeps, press Keep Warm/Cancel. Allow the Instant Pot to release its pressure naturally for 15 minutes. Using an oven mitt, open the steam-release valve. If there is any steam left over, allow it to release until the silver dial drops, then carefully open the lid.

Carefully remove the pork roast, place it on a large plate or cutting board and pull it apart into shreds. Transfer the shredded pork back to the Instant Pot, then add the blueberries and blackberries and stir to combine, making sure all the pork gets coated. Place the lid back on the Instant Pot, making sure the steam-release valve is sealed. Press the Manual button and set the Instant Pot for 5 minutes.

When the Instant Pot beeps, press Keep Warm/Cancel. Using an oven mitt, "quick release" the steam-release valve. When the steam stops venting and the silver dial drops, carefully open the lid.

Stir the shredded pork several times, until everything is fully incorporated. Transfer the shredded berry pork to a shallow dish and allow the juices to set and absorb into the meat for 10 minutes.

Serve the pork immediately or refrigerate it for later use.

NOTE: Don't forget to keep the size of your Instant Pot in mind when purchasing the pork roast.

MEDITERRANEAN LAMB-STUFFED BELL PEPPERS

PREP TIME: 25 MINUTES
COOK TIME: 24 MINUTES
TOTAL TIME: 49 MINUTES
YIELD: 4 SERVINGS

These bell pepper cornucopias, magnificently stuffed with the radiant presence of mint, olives and zesty lemon, embody visions of Greece. Let the Instant Pot bring these vibrant flavors to your table, with hardly any time or effort on your part.

2 tbsp (30 g) grass-fed butter or ghee or 2 tbsp (30 ml) avocado oil, plus more as needed

½ cup (35 g) finely chopped mushrooms

4 cloves garlic, minced

2 scallions (white and light green parts only), finely chopped

1 lb (454 g) ground lamb

1 large egg

1 tsp sea salt

Zest of 1 lemon

1 small zucchini, grated

¾ cup (45 g) finely chopped fresh mint

½ cup (30 g) finely chopped fresh Italian parsley

¼ tsp freshly ground black pepper

½ cup (80 g) coarsely chopped Kalamata or green olives

½ cup (50 g) shredded Parmesan cheese

¼ cup (38 g) crumbled feta cheese

4 large red or orange bell peppers, tops and seeds removed

1 cup (240 ml) filtered water

Add the butter to the Instant Pot and press Sauté. Once the butter has melted, add the mushrooms and sauté for 7 minutes, stirring occasionally. Add the garlic and scallions and sauté for 2 minutes, stirring occasionally. Press Keep Warm/Cancel.

Using additional butter, grease a 1½-quart (1.5-L) baking dish with a glass lid that fits in the Instant Pot. Set aside.

In a large bowl, combine the lamb, egg, salt, lemon zest, zucchini, mint, parsley, black pepper, olives, Parmesan cheese, feta cheese and the mushroom mixture. Gently mix until everything is combined. Evenly divide the filling among the bell peppers. Transfer the stuffed bell peppers to the baking dish. Place the lid on top of the baking dish.

Place the Instant Pot trivet inside the Instant Pot. Pour the water into the Instant Pot. Carefully transfer the covered baking dish to the Instant Pot on top of the trivet.

Place the lid on the Instant Pot, making sure the steam-release valve is sealed. Press the Manual button and set the Instant Pot for 15 minutes.

When the Instant Pot beeps, press Keep Warm/Cancel. Using an oven mitt, "quick release" the steam-release valve. When the steam stops venting and the silver dial drops, carefully open the lid.

Carefully remove the baking dish from the Instant Pot and remove the lid.

Serve immediately.

NOTES: If you don't have a lid for your baking dish, you can place a piece of parchment paper over the top of the baking dish, then cover it securely with foil.

If you don't care for lamb, ground beef or ground poultry can be substituted.

SPAGHETTI SQUASH AND MEATBALLS

PREP TIME: 25 MINUTES
COOK TIME: 24 MINUTES
TOTAL TIME: 49 MINUTES
YIELD: 4 TO 6 SERVINGS

Spaghetti and meatballs—comfort food at its finest, minus the carb-heavy pasta! This is a nice alternative to the traditional pasta dish. It's still full of flavor and just as satisfying, except instead of all that spaghetti, you'll get a nice serving of healthy squash instead.

MEATBALLS

1 lb (454 g) ground beef

¼ cup (19 g) finely chopped mushrooms

1 celery rib, finely chopped

1½ tsp (5 g) granulated garlic or garlic powder

½ tsp onion powder

1 tsp sea salt

¼ cup (15 g) finely chopped fresh Italian parsley

½ tsp dried oregano

1 large egg

SAUCE

3 tbsp (45 g) grass-fed butter or ghee or 3 tbsp (45 ml) avocado oil

½ small onion, diced

4 cloves garlic, minced

1 tsp fresh thyme leaves

36 oz (1.1 L) crushed tomatoes

¼ cup (60 ml) dry red wine

½ cup (120 ml) heavy cream

¼ cup (15 g) finely chopped fresh Italian parsley

¼ cup (15 g) fresh basil, finely chopped

Zest of 1 lemon

1 tsp sea salt

½ cup (50 g) shredded Parmesan cheese, plus more as needed

1 large spaghetti squash (see Notes)

To make the meatballs, in a mixing bowl, combine the beef, mushrooms, celery, granulated garlic, onion powder, salt, parsley, oregano and egg. Gently mix until everything is evenly distributed and combined. Roll the mixture into meatballs about 2 inches (5 cm) in diameter. Set them aside on a plate.

To make the sauce, add the butter to the Instant Pot and press Sauté. Once the butter has melted, add the onion and sauté for 7 minutes, stirring occasionally. Add the garlic and thyme and sauté for 2 minutes, stirring occasionally. Add the tomatoes, wine, cream, parsley, basil, lemon zest, salt and Parmesan cheese, then stir until combined. Press Keep Warm/Cancel.

Wash the outside of the spaghetti squash and use a sharp knife to puncture the squash all over. Gently place the meatballs in the Instant Pot, making sure they're submerged in the sauce, or use a spoon to coat them with the sauce, taking care not to break them apart. Set the spaghetti squash on top of the sauce and meatballs.

Place the lid on the Instant Pot, making sure the steam-release valve is sealed. Press the Manual button and set the Instant Pot for 15 minutes.

When the Instant Pot beeps, press Keep Warm/Cancel. Using an oven mitt, "quick release" the steam-release valve. When the steam stops venting and the silver dial drops, carefully open the lid.

Remove the squash with tongs and place it on a plate or cutting board. Cut the squash in half widthwise (see Notes). Use a spoon to scrape out the seeds and stringy parts, then discard them. Use a fork to scrape out the strands of spaghetti squash. Set them aside.

Add the spaghetti squash strands to a serving plate, then ladle the sauce and meatballs over the top. Serve immediately, garnished with additional Parmesan.

NOTES: Ensure that the spaghetti squash you purchase can fit whole inside your Instant Pot. If a large squash won't fit, use a medium one.

Alternatively, you can cut the squash lengthwise, but I prefer to cut it widthwise because you will get longer strands of "spaghetti" compared to the shorter strands you get when you cut it lengthwise.

SPICY BUFFALO CHICKEN WINGS

INACTIVE PREP TIME: 20 MINUTES
PREP TIME: 15 MINUTES
COOK TIME: 19 MINUTES
TOTAL TIME: 54 MINUTES
YIELD: 4 TO 6 SERVINGS

Buffalo wings are all the rage these days. People love these spicy chicken bites, which are doused with hot sauce and served with a dipping sauce or crumbled blue cheese. In our recipe, the wings get a bath in a homemade hot sauce marinade before being cooked with a bunch of butter—the finished result is lip-smacking good.

4 oz (112 g) cayenne peppers, stems removed

¼ cup (60 ml) apple cider vinegar

1 tsp granulated garlic or garlic powder

½ tsp smoked paprika or paprika

1 tsp granulated erythritol

Zest of 1 orange

½ tsp sea salt

3 lb (1.4 kg) chicken wings

8 tbsp (120 g) grass-fed butter

½ cup (75 g) crumbled blue cheese

In a blender, combine the cayenne peppers, vinegar, granulated garlic, smoked paprika, erythritol, orange zest and salt and then pulse until the ingredients are completely pureed. Transfer the sauce to a large bowl. Add the chicken wings, stirring to coat, and allow them to marinate for 20 minutes.

Add the butter to the Instant Pot and press Sauté. Once the butter has melted, press Keep Warm/Cancel.

Add the chicken wings along with the sauce to the Instant Pot. Stir to combine.

Place the lid on the Instant Pot, making sure the steam-release valve is sealed. Press the Manual button, and set the Instant Pot for 13 minutes.

When the Instant Pot beeps, press Keep Warm/Cancel. Allow the Instant Pot to release its pressure naturally for 15 minutes. Using an oven mitt, open the steam-release valve. If there is any steam left over, allow it to release until the silver dial drops, then carefully open the lid.

While the Instant Pot is releasing its pressure, preheat the oven to broil.

Carefully transfer the chicken wings to a large baking sheet and place it on the middle oven rack for 2 to 3 minutes, to lightly brown and crisp the skin. Don't walk away; the wings can burn quickly. Flip the wings over and broil for 2 to 3 minutes.

Serve the wings immediately with the blue cheese.

NOTE: Alternatively, you can use 3 teaspoons (5 g) cayenne pepper instead of fresh cayenne peppers. Cayenne peppers are easier to find at most natural-foods stores, Asian markets and some local farmers' markets.

HIGH-FAT ARTICHOKE DIP

PREP TIME: 25 MINUTES
COOK TIME: 12 MINUTES
TOTAL TIME: 37 MINUTES
YIELD: 4 TO 6 SERVINGS

My husband and I love cheesy artichoke dip! Our little one does too—she'll devour it. This scrumptious comfort food is so fun to share with those you love, so grab some spoons and your favorite low-carb veggie chips, homemade low-carb flatbread or low-carb "tortilla chips" and dig in.

Grass-fed butter, as needed

16 oz (454 g) jarred or canned artichoke hearts (not marinated), drained and coarsely chopped

4 oz (113 g) cream cheese, softened

1 cup (230 g) sour cream

1 cup (111 g) shredded mozzarella cheese

1 cup (113 g) shredded Monterey Jack or pepper Jack cheese

¾ cup (75 g) shredded Parmesan cheese, divided

Zest of 1 lemon

2 tbsp (30 ml) fresh lemon juice

1 tsp sea salt

1½ tsp (5 g) granulated garlic or garlic powder

3 scallions (white and light green parts only), finely chopped

½ cup (30 g) finely chopped fresh Italian parsley

1 cup (240 ml) filtered water

With butter, grease a 1½-quart (1.5-L) baking dish with a glass lid that fits in the Instant Pot. Set aside.

In a large bowl, combine the artichoke hearts, cream cheese, sour cream, mozzarella cheese, Monterey Jack cheese, ½ cup (50 g) of the Parmesan cheese, lemon zest, lemon juice, salt, granulated garlic, scallions and parsley, stirring until the ingredients are thoroughly mixed.

Add the artichoke dip mixture to the prepared baking dish. Evenly sprinkle the remaining ¼ cup (25 g) Parmesan cheese on top of the dip. Place the glass lid on top of the baking dish.

Place the Instant Pot trivet inside the Instant Pot. Pour the water into the Instant Pot. Carefully transfer the covered baking dish to the Instant Pot on top of the trivet.

Place the lid on the Instant Pot, making sure the steam-release valve is sealed. Press the Manual button, and set the Instant Pot for 10 minutes.

When the Instant Pot beeps, press Keep Warm/Cancel. Using an oven mitt, "quick release" the steam-release valve. When the steam stops venting and the silver dial drops, carefully open the lid.

Carefully remove the baking dish from the Instant Pot and remove the dish's lid. Serve immediately.

Alternatively, if you prefer a browned top, place the baking dish on a small baking sheet and place under a preheated broiler for 1 to 2 minutes, just until the top becomes bubbly and the Parmesan cheese is golden brown, then serve immediately.

NOTE: If you don't have a lid for your baking dish, you can place a piece of parchment paper over the top, then cover it securely with foil.

LOW-CARB GREEN BEAN CASSEROLE

PREP TIME: 25 MINUTES
COOK TIME: 13 MINUTES
TOTAL TIME: 38 MINUTES
YIELD: 4 TO 6 SERVINGS

Most of us grew up enjoying this side dish topped with crispy deep-fried breaded onions, but the original recipe is gluten-heavy and packed with canned ingredients. You won't find any onion rings, canned beans or canned soup in this low-carb version, so go ahead and enjoy this classic casserole—the holidays are not the same without it!

3 tbsp (45 g) grass-fed butter

8 oz (224 g) mushrooms, cut into thirds, woody ends removed

3 cloves garlic, finely chopped

1 cup (240 ml) Homemade Cream of Mushroom Soup (page 97)

1½ lb (680 g) fresh green beans, trimmed

8 oz (224 g) cream cheese, softened

½ cup (115 g) sour cream

½ cup (30 g) finely chopped fresh Italian parsley

Zest of 1 lemon

1 tsp sea salt

¾ tsp onion powder

¼ tsp freshly ground black pepper

¾ cup (83 g) shredded mozzarella cheese

¾ cup (90 g) shredded cheddar cheese

¾ cup (75 g) shredded Parmesan cheese, divided

9 pieces crispy cooked bacon, crumbled

Add the butter to the Instant Pot and press Sauté. Once the butter has melted, add the mushrooms and sauté for 7 minutes, stirring occasionally, until the mushrooms have begun to caramelize and turn golden brown. Add the garlic, stir and sauté for 1 minute. Press Keep Warm/Cancel.

Add the cream of mushroom soup, green beans, cream cheese, sour cream, parsley, lemon zest, salt, onion powder and black pepper to the Instant Pot, then stir until the cream cheese is incorporated.

Place the lid on the Instant Pot, making sure the steam-release valve is sealed. Press the Manual button and set the Instant Pot for 5 minutes.

When the Instant Pot beeps, press Keep Warm/Cancel. Using an oven mitt, "quick release" the steam-release valve. When the steam stops venting and the silver dial drops, carefully open the lid.

Add the mozzarella cheese, cheddar cheese and Parmesan cheese and stir until they're completely incorporated.

Transfer the green bean casserole to a serving dish and top with the bacon. Serve immediately.

QUICK LOW-CARB WEEKNIGHT MEALS

Banish the pressure of meal prep from your weekend, and carb-laden foods from your plate with these quick and easy low-carb meals. Simply toss a handful of ingredients in the Instant Pot and press Start to eliminate the weeknight-dinner limbo of what to have and where to go and—even better—to enjoy a tasty, healthier meal in the same time it would take to order fast food or takeout.

You won't have to worry about what the neighborhood restaurant is putting in their food (like unhealthy oils and grains) when you can make our healthier Takeout-at-Home Asian Chicken and Broccoli (page 33).

Or if it's more of an upscale dining experience you're seeking, enjoy Healthy Alaskan Cod with Tomato-Olive Tapenade (page 61) or Sweet and Spicy Shredded Blackberry Ham (page 34).

It's human nature to want good food fast—do yourself and your body a favor by putting nourishing, low-carb ingredients and healthier fats in an Instant Pot to make delicious meals even faster and better for you.

TAKEOUT-AT-HOME ASIAN CHICKEN AND BROCCOLI

PREP TIME: 25 MINUTES
COOK TIME: 20 MINUTES
TOTAL TIME: 45 MINUTES
YIELD: 3 TO 4 SERVINGS

There's no need to order takeout when you're in a pinch for time, because the Instant Pot helps make "take-out-at-home" so easy! This Asian-inspired dish is packed with warming flavors like ginger and five-spice seasoning, with a touch of nuttiness and tangy sweetness. It's delicious served with sautéed riced cauliflower too.

3 tbsp (45 ml) toasted sesame oil

5 boneless and skinless chicken thighs, cut into 2-inch (5-cm) cubes

4 cloves garlic, finely chopped

1-inch (2.5-cm) piece fresh ginger, peeled and minced or grated

3 scallions (white and light green parts only), finely chopped, plus more as needed

½ tsp five-spice powder

2 tbsp (30 ml) apple cider vinegar

½ cup (120 ml) chicken broth

1 tbsp (15 ml) coconut aminos or liquid aminos

1 tsp sea salt

1 tbsp (8 g) powdered erythritol

3 small heads broccoli, cut into florets

2 tsp (6 g) toasted sesame seeds

Add the oil to the Instant Pot and press Sauté. Once the oil is hot, add the chicken and sauté for 7 minutes, stirring occasionally, until the chicken is browned on most sides. Add the garlic, ginger, scallions and five-spice powder and sauté for 2 minutes until fragrant, stirring occasionally. Add the vinegar, chicken broth, coconut aminos, salt and erythritol, stirring until the ingredients are incorporated. Press Keep Warm/Cancel.

Add the broccoli to the Instant Pot, gently stirring until mostly incorporated.

Place the lid on the Instant Pot, making sure the steam-release valve is sealed. Press the Manual button and set the Instant Pot for 6 minutes.

When the Instant Pot beeps, press Keep Warm/Cancel. Allow the Instant Pot to release its pressure naturally for 10 minutes. Using an oven mitt, open the steam-release valve. If there is any steam left over, allow it to release until the silver dial drops, then carefully open the lid.

Press Sauté and allow the sauce to come to a boil, then simmer for 3 to 5 minutes to allow the sauce to thicken. Press Keep Warm/Cancel and allow the chicken and broccoli to rest for 10 minutes before serving. The sauce will thicken more as it rests.

Serve immediately, garnished with additional scallions and the sesame seeds.

NOTE: Five-spice powder is a spice blend that is easy to find at mainstream grocery stores as well as natural-foods stores and Asian markets.

SWEET AND SPICY SHREDDED BLACKBERRY HAM

PREP TIME: 25 MINUTES
COOK TIME: 65 MINUTES
TOTAL TIME: 90 MINUTES
YIELD: 10 TO 12 SERVINGS

My husband and I grew up enjoying Honey Baked Ham, usually on holidays like Thanksgiving, Christmas and Easter. This was actually the only time I liked ham, because the sweet honey flavor was so good. Now we love making low-carb versions of that highly-sugared dish, like this festive sugar-free sweet and spicy shredded ham.

1 (3-lb [1.4-kg]) half-cut cooked boneless ham (not spiral), cut into 2-inch (5-cm) chunks

3 cups (720 ml) filtered water

1 cup (240 ml) apple cider vinegar

½ cup (100 g) granulated erythritol

½ tsp ground allspice

2 cups (288 g) fresh or frozen blackberries

1 small jalapeño, stems and seeds removed, finely diced

2 tbsp (30 ml) yacon syrup or erythritol- and monk fruit-based maple syrup

Place the ham in the Instant Pot. Cover the ham with the water, vinegar, erythritol and allspice. If your ham isn't fully covered, add more water and vinegar, being careful not to exceed the maximum fill line. Place the lid on the Instant Pot, making sure the steam-release valve is sealed. Press the Manual button and set the Instant Pot for 35 minutes.

When the Instant Pot beeps, press Keep Warm/Cancel. Using an oven mitt, "quick release" the steam-release valve. When the steam stops venting and the silver dial drops, carefully open the lid.

Carefully remove the ham chunks, place them on a large plate or cutting board and pull them apart into shredded pieces. Pour the cooking liquid out of the Instant Pot and discard it. Add the shredded ham back to the Instant Pot, then add the blackberries, jalapeño and yacon syrup and stir to combine, making sure all the ham gets coated. Place the lid back on the Instant Pot, making sure the steam-release valve is sealed. Set the Keep Warm/Cancel setting for 30 minutes. After the ham has warmed for 30 minutes, press Keep Warm/Cancel and turn off the Instant Pot. Use an oven mitt to open the steam-release valve.

Stir the ham several times, until everything is fully incorporated. Pour the ham into a shallow serving dish and let it rest for 10 minutes to allow the juices to set up and absorb into the ham.

Serve the ham immediately or chill it and serve cold.

NOTE: Yacon syrup and erythritol- and monk fruit–based maple syrup can be found in some larger natural-foods stores and easily found online.

GARLIC-BUTTER LOBSTER TAILS

PREP TIME: 15 MINUTES
COOK TIME: 6 MINUTES
TOTAL TIME: 21 MINUTES
YIELD: 2 TO 4 SERVINGS

Succulent lobster dipped in garlicky melted butter and drizzled with fresh lemon juice: Now that's a special meal! Lobster tails are much more affordable than a whole lobster, and today they're available in the freezer sections of most grocery stores. Enjoy this seemingly fancy yet simple treat with someone you love.

1 cup (240 ml) filtered water

4 (5- to 6-oz [140- to 168-g]) fresh or frozen lobster tails

6 tbsp (90 g) grass-fed butter, melted

2 cloves garlic, finely chopped

2 tbsp (10 g) finely chopped fresh Italian parsley (optional)

1 tbsp (5 g) finely chopped fresh dill (optional)

Lemon wedges

Add the water to the Instant Pot. Place the Instant Pot trivet inside the pot so it's sitting above the water. Place the lobster tails, shell side down, on top of the trivet.

Place the lid on the Instant Pot, making sure the steam-release valve is sealed. Press the Manual button and set the Instant Pot for 3 minutes if the lobster tails are fresh. If the lobster tails are frozen, press the Manual button and set the Instant Pot for 4 minutes.

When the Instant Pot beeps, press Keep Warm/Cancel. Using an oven mitt, "quick release" the steam-release valve. When the steam stops venting and the silver dial drops, carefully open the lid. Using tongs, transfer the lobster tails to a plate.

In a small pot over medium heat, combine the butter and garlic, allowing the garlic to cook for about 2 minutes, just until fragrant. Add the parsley and dill, if using, and stir to combine.

Serve the lobster tails immediately with the garlic butter and lemon wedges.

HIGH-FAT HERB-BUTTER SALMON

PREP TIME: **15 MINUTES**
COOK TIME: **4 MINUTES**
TOTAL TIME: **19 MINUTES**
YIELD: **2 SERVINGS**

This delicate salmon is infused with aromatics and finished with an enticing herbed compound butter. If you've never made a compound butter before, it's simply a mixture of butter and other ingredients, which can be savory or sweet. These special butters can be used to add an extra pop of flavor on top of meats, vegetables or even low-carb baked goods.

1 cup (240 ml) filtered water

2 sprigs fresh Italian parsley

3 sprigs fresh dill

5 cloves garlic, crushed

1 (1-lb [454-g]) wild-caught, skin-on Alaskan salmon fillet

5 tbsp (75 g) grass-fed butter, softened, divided

¾ tsp sea salt

1 tsp granulated garlic

1 tbsp (5 g) finely chopped fresh Italian parsley

1 tbsp (5 g) finely chopped fresh dill

1 tsp finely chopped fresh chives

Add the water, parsley sprigs, dill sprigs and garlic to the Instant Pot. Place the Instant Pot trivet inside the pot so it's sitting above the water.

Place the salmon, skin side down, on top of the trivet. Place 1 tablespoon (15 g) of the butter on top of the salmon. Sprinkle the salt and granulated garlic over the salmon.

Place the lid on the Instant Pot, making sure the steam-release valve is sealed. Press the Manual button, and set the Instant Pot for 4 minutes.

When the Instant Pot beeps, press Keep Warm/Cancel. Using an oven mitt, "quick release" the steam-release valve. When the steam stops venting and the silver dial drops, carefully open the lid.

While the Instant Pot is releasing its pressure, preheat the oven to broil.

Using oven mitts, carefully remove the trivet with the salmon on it from the Instant Pot. Set the trivet on a plate and check the salmon for doneness. If you prefer a crispier salmon, carefully place the salmon on a medium baking sheet and place it under the broiler for 1 to 2 minutes, just until lightly browned, watching it closely to prevent burning. Discard the cooking liquid, parsley sprigs, dill sprigs and garlic.

Place the remaining 4 tablespoons (60 g) of butter in a small bowl. Add the chopped parsley, chopped dill and chopped chives to the butter and mash or stir until the herbs are fully incorporated into the butter.

Top the hot salmon with the herb butter, evenly distributing the butter as it melts. Serve immediately.

NOTE: If your salmon fillet is thicker in some areas, you may need to increase the cook time by 1 minute.

HALIBUT WITH SWEET STRAWBERRY COMPOTE

PREP TIME: **15 MINUTES**
COOK TIME: **14 MINUTES**
TOTAL TIME: **29 MINUTES**
YIELD: **2 SERVINGS**

Halibut is one of our favorites because it's easy to prepare and doesn't have that strong sea taste. This dish is inspired by a meal I had in my teens. It was so good that it left a lasting impression and this is our re-creation of it. This tender, basil-infused halibut is garnished with a sweet strawberry compote and is simply exquisite.

8 oz (224 g) fresh or frozen strawberries

1 tbsp (16 g) granulated erythritol

1 cup (240 ml) dry white wine

12 fresh basil leaves

5 cloves garlic, crushed

1 (1-lb [454-g]) wild-caught, skin-on halibut fillet

2 tbsp (30 g) grass-fed butter, divided

¾ tsp sea salt

1 tsp granulated garlic

2 tbsp (10 g) finely chopped fresh basil (optional)

Place the strawberries and erythritol in a small pot over medium heat, stirring occasionally for about 10 minutes, or just until the berries break down and create a thick sauce. Pour the compote into a heatproof bowl and chill it in the refrigerator until ready to serve.

Place the wine, basil and crushed garlic into the Instant Pot. Place the Instant Pot trivet inside the pot so it's sitting above the wine. Place the halibut, skin side down, on top of the trivet. Add 1 tablespoon (15 g) of the butter on top of the halibut. Sprinkle the salt and granulated garlic over the halibut.

Place the lid on the Instant Pot, making sure the steam-release valve is sealed. Press the Manual button, and set the Instant Pot for 4 minutes.

When the Instant Pot beeps, press Keep Warm/Cancel. Using an oven mitt, "quick release" the steam-release valve. When the steam stops venting and the silver dial drops, carefully open the lid.

Using oven mitts, carefully remove the trivet with the halibut on it from the Instant Pot. Set the trivet on a plate and check the halibut for doneness. If you prefer a crispier skin, carefully place the halibut on a medium baking sheet and place it under a preheated broiler for 1 to 2 minutes, just until lightly browned, watching it closely to prevent burning. Discard the cooking liquid, basil leaves and crushed garlic.

Top the hot halibut with the remaining 1 tablespoon (15 g) butter, evenly distributing the butter across the fillet as it melts. Garnish the halibut with the strawberry compote and chopped basil, if using. Serve immediately.

NOTES: If your halibut fillet is thicker in some areas, you may need to increase the cook time by 1 minute.

This fish is delicious served with Low-Carb Turnip and Celery Root Mash (page 133), Caramelized Fennel and Turnips (page 146) or Garlic-Herb Brussels Sprouts (page 138). No-Sugar Rhubarb Compote (page 158) can also be substituted for the strawberry compote.

SCALLION-GINGER ASIAN MEATBALLS

PREP TIME: 25 MINUTES
COOK TIME: 15 MINUTES
TOTAL TIME: 40 MINUTES
YIELD: 4 TO 6 SERVINGS

Meatballs are always a fun crowd-pleaser. These Asian-inspired meatballs are packed with scallions and ginger and "braised" in a coconut-garlic-ginger broth. The best part is that these tasty little bites cook quickly in the Instant Pot, which locks in their juices and keeps them tender.

1 lb (454 g) ground beef

1 large egg

¼ cup (19 g) finely chopped mushrooms

3 scallions (white and light green parts only), finely chopped

1½ tsp (5 g) granulated garlic or garlic powder

1 tsp ground ginger

1 tsp sea salt

½ tsp freshly ground black pepper

¼ cup (15 g) finely chopped fresh Italian parsley

¼ cup (15 g) finely chopped fresh cilantro

2 tsp (10 ml) coconut aminos or liquid aminos

2 tbsp (30 g) ghee or 2 tbsp (30 ml) avocado oil

½ cup (120 ml) coconut water

2 cloves garlic, crushed

1 (½-inch [13-mm]) piece fresh ginger, peeled and finely chopped or grated

In a large bowl, combine the ground beef, egg, mushrooms, scallions, granulated garlic, ginger, salt, pepper, parsley, cilantro and aminos. Gently mix until everything is evenly distributed. Roll the mixture into small meatballs about 1 inch (2.5 cm) in diameter. Set them aside on a plate.

Add the ghee to the Instant Pot and press Sauté. Once the ghee has melted, working in batches, add the meatballs and brown them on each side, about 1 minute per side. Set aside the browned meatballs on another plate. Press Keep Warm/Cancel.

Add the coconut water, crushed garlic and fresh ginger to the Instant Pot. Gently add the meatballs to the Instant Pot, making sure to ladle some of the liquid over the meatballs.

Place the lid on the Instant Pot, making sure the steam-release valve is sealed. Press the Manual button and set the Instant Pot for 13 minutes.

When the Instant Pot beeps, press Keep Warm/Cancel. Using an oven mitt, "quick release" the steam-release valve. When the steam stops venting and the silver dial drops, carefully open the lid.

Serve immediately.

NOTE: If you don't care for ground beef, ground poultry can be substituted.

SUN-DRIED TOMATO PESTO SALMON

PREP TIME: **25 MINUTES**
COOK TIME: **4 MINUTES**
TOTAL TIME: **29 MINUTES**
YIELD: **2 SERVINGS**

There's nothing like salty sun-dried tomatoes paired with vibrant, refreshing pesto. This bright, lemony salmon cooks perfectly in the Instant Pot in minutes, and it's topped with a mouthwatering sun-dried tomato pesto.

SUN-DRIED TOMATO PESTO

7 sun-dried tomatoes packed in olive oil

1 cup (24 g) fresh basil leaves, stems removed

1 tbsp (5 g) finely chopped fresh Italian parsley

1 clove garlic, crushed

Zest of 1 lemon

2 tbsp (30 ml) fresh lemon juice

2 tbsp (30 ml) extra virgin olive oil

3 oz (85 g) Parmesan cheese, cut into chunks

¼ tsp sea salt

SALMON

1 cup (240 ml) filtered water

10 thin lemon slices, divided

2 sprigs fresh Italian parsley

3 fresh basil leaves

5 cloves garlic, crushed

1 (1-lb [454-g]) wild-caught, skin-on Alaskan salmon fillet

1 tbsp (15 g) grass-fed butter

¾ tsp sea salt

1 tsp granulated garlic

To make the sun-dried tomato pesto, combine the sun-dried tomatoes, basil, parsley, garlic, lemon zest, lemon juice, oil, Parmesan and salt in a food processor. Pulse until fully combined and smooth, about 30 seconds. Taste for seasoning and add more salt if needed. Store the pesto in the refrigerator until ready to use.

To make the salmon, place the water, four of the lemon slices, parsley, basil and crushed garlic in the Instant Pot. Place the Instant Pot trivet inside the pot so it's sitting above the water.

Place the salmon, skin side down, on top of the trivet. Place the butter on top of the salmon. Sprinkle the salt and granulated garlic over the salmon. Place the remaining six lemon slices on the top of the salmon.

Place the lid on the Instant Pot, making sure the steam-release valve is sealed. Press the Manual button and set the Instant Pot for 4 minutes.

When the Instant Pot beeps, press Keep Warm/Cancel. Using an oven mitt, "quick release" the steam-release valve. When the steam stops venting and the silver dial drops, carefully open the lid.

Using oven mitts, carefully remove the trivet with the salmon on it from the Instant Pot. Set the trivet on a plate and check the salmon for doneness. If you prefer a crispier salmon, carefully place the salmon on a medium baking sheet and place it under a preheated broiler for 1 to 2 minutes, just until lightly browned, watching it closely to prevent burning. Discard the cooking liquid, four lemon slices, parsley, basil and crushed garlic.

Leave the lemons on the top of the salmon or discard them as desired. Top the salmon with the sun-dried tomato pesto. Serve immediately.

NOTES: Avocado oil or ghee can be used as a substitute for the butter if needed. If your salmon fillet is thicker in some areas, you may need to increase the cook time by 1 minute.

SIMPLE STEAMED CRAB LEGS

PREP TIME: 15 MINUTES
COOK TIME: 6 MINUTES
TOTAL TIME: 21 MINUTES
YIELD: 2 TO 3 SERVINGS

It's easy to make a feast of crab legs with your Instant Pot because it cooks them so efficiently and quickly. Crab has been a favorite of mine ever since I was a little girl, but we had it only on special occasions, like when we visited Bodega Bay, California, or once in a blue moon during crab season. My mom would always make our simple crab meals feel like a magical feast. Our favorite way to serve it is with melted butter and lemon wedges.

CRAB LEGS

1 cup (240 ml) filtered water

3 lb (1.4 kg) Alaskan crab legs

Fresh lemon wedges

GARLIC-HERB BUTTER (OPTIONAL)

6 tbsp (90 g) grass-fed butter, melted

1 clove garlic, finely chopped

2 tbsp (10 g) finely chopped fresh Italian parsley

To make the crab legs, add the water to the Instant Pot. Place the Instant Pot trivet inside the pot so it's sitting above the water. Place the crab legs on top of the trivet.

Place the lid on the Instant Pot, making sure the steam-release valve is sealed. Press the Manual button and set the Instant Pot for 4 minutes.

When the Instant Pot beeps, press Keep Warm/Cancel. Using an oven mitt, "quick release" the steam-release valve. When the steam stops venting and the silver dial drops, carefully open the lid.

If desired, make the garlic-herb butter. In a small pot over medium heat, combine the butter and garlic, allowing the garlic to cook for about 2 minutes, just until fragrant. Add the parsley and stir.

Serve the crab legs immediately with plain butter or the garlic-herb butter, if using, and the lemon wedges.

SAVORY RANCH CHICKEN

PREP TIME: 25 MINUTES
COOK TIME: 15 MINUTES
TOTAL TIME: 40 MINUTES
YIELD: 3 TO 4 SERVINGS

Ranch is an incredibly popular dressing, and most people go crazy for that herbaceous taste. Bursting with ranch flavor, this tasty chicken dish is so easy and quick to make. You're going to love these delicious little bites of chicken!

3 tbsp (45 g) grass-fed butter or ghee

3 (4-oz [112-g]) boneless and skinless chicken breasts, cut into 1½-inch (4-cm) cubes

1 tbsp (3 g) dried dill

1 tsp sea salt

1 tsp granulated garlic or garlic powder

½ tsp onion powder

½ tsp ground mustard

½ tsp paprika

¼ tsp freshly ground black pepper

Zest of 1 lemon

¼ cup (15 g) finely chopped fresh Italian parsley, plus more as needed

1 tbsp (5 g) finely chopped fresh chives, plus more as needed

¼ cup (60 ml) chicken broth

½ cup (120 ml) heavy cream

1 cup (240 g) cream cheese, softened

¾ cup (75 g) shredded Parmesan cheese

Add the butter to the Instant Pot and press Sauté. Once the butter has melted, add the chicken and sauté for 7 minutes, stirring occasionally, until the chicken is browned on most sides. Add the dill, salt, granulated garlic, onion powder, mustard, paprika, pepper, lemon zest, parsley and chives, stirring to combine. Press Keep Warm/Cancel.

Add the chicken broth, heavy cream and cream cheese to the Instant Pot, stirring until mostly incorporated.

Place the lid on the Instant Pot, making sure the steam-release valve is sealed. Press the Manual button and set the Instant Pot for 8 minutes.

When the Instant Pot beeps, press Keep Warm/Cancel. Allow the Instant Pot to release its pressure naturally for 10 minutes. Using an oven mitt, open the steam-release valve. If there is any steam left over, allow it to release until the silver dial drops, then carefully open the lid.

Add the Parmesan cheese to the Instant Pot, stirring until it is fully incorporated.

Serve immediately, garnished with additional parsley and chives, if desired.

MEDITERRANEAN WHITEFISH WITH TOMATO-CUCUMBER SALSA

PREP TIME: **25 MINUTES**
COOK TIME: **4 MINUTES**
TOTAL TIME: **29 MINUTES**
YIELD: **2 SERVINGS**

Salsa is usually tomato-heavy, but not this one! The cucumber adds the most refreshing flavor to this appetizing salsa. It goes perfectly with this simple whitefish meal, which you can cook in no time.

TOMATO-CUCUMBER SALSA

1 medium tomato, cut into large chunks

½ small cucumber, peeled and cut into large chunks

½ cup (16 g) fresh cilantro

1 small jalapeño, halved, stems and seeds removed

2 cloves garlic, crushed

2 tbsp (30 ml) fresh lemon juice

¼ tsp sea salt

WHITEFISH

1 cup (240 ml) filtered water

10 thin lemon slices, divided

2 sprigs fresh Italian parsley

5 cloves garlic, crushed

1 (1-lb [454-g]) wild-caught, skin-on whitefish fillet

2 tbsp (30 g) grass-fed butter, divided

¾ tsp sea salt

1 tsp granulated garlic

To make the tomato-cucumber salsa, combine the tomato, cucumber, cilantro, jalapeño, garlic, lemon juice and salt in a food processor. Pulse until the ingredients are combined but still retain some texture, about 15 seconds. Taste the salsa for seasoning and add more salt if needed. Store the salsa in the refrigerator until ready to use.

To make the whitefish, add the water, four of the lemon slices, parsley sprigs and crushed garlic to the Instant Pot. Place the Instant Pot trivet inside the pot so it's sitting above the water. Place the whitefish, skin side down, on top of the trivet. Place 1 tablespoon (15 g) of the butter on top of the fish, then sprinkle the salt and granulated garlic. Place the remaining six lemon slices on the top of the fish.

Place the lid on the Instant Pot, making sure the steam-release valve is sealed. Press the Manual button and set the Instant Pot for 4 minutes.

When the Instant Pot beeps, press Keep Warm/Cancel. Using an oven mitt, "quick release" the steam-release valve. When the steam stops venting and the silver dial drops, carefully open the lid.

Carefully remove the trivet with the whitefish on it from the Instant Pot. Set the trivet on a plate and check the fish for doneness. If you prefer a crispier fish, carefully place the fish on a medium baking sheet and place it under a preheated broiler for 1 to 2 minutes, just until lightly browned, watching it closely to prevent burning. Discard the cooking liquid, four lemon slices, parsley and garlic.

Leave the lemons on the top of the fish or discard them as desired. Top the hot fish with the remaining 1 tablespoon (15 g) butter, evenly distributing the butter as it melts. Garnish the fish with the tomato-cucumber salsa. Serve immediately.

NOTES: Cod, halibut or another flaky whitefish can be used in this recipe. Avocado oil or ghee can be used as a substitute for the butter if needed. If your fish is thicker in some areas, you may need to increase the cook time by 1 minute. If the fish is very thin, reduce the cooking time by 1 minute.

GARLIC-SCALLION SALMON

PREP TIME: **15 MINUTES**
COOK TIME: **4 MINUTES**
TOTAL TIME: **19 MINUTES**
YIELD: **2 SERVINGS**

Salmon is one of the easiest things to cook in the Instant Pot, and best of all, it cooks super fast! Before you know it, you'll be enjoying this delicious garlic- and scallion-infused, buttery salmon.

1 cup (240 ml) filtered water

5 scallions, divided

5 cloves garlic, crushed

1 (1-lb [454-g]) wild-caught, skin-on Alaskan salmon fillet

2 tbsp (30 g) grass-fed butter, divided

¾ tsp sea salt

1 tsp granulated garlic

¼ cup (15 g) finely chopped Italian parsley (optional)

Place the water, three scallions and crushed garlic in the Instant Pot. Place the Instant Pot trivet inside the pot so it's sitting above the water.

Place the salmon, skin side down, on top of the trivet. Place 1 tablespoon (15 g) of the butter on top of the salmon. Sprinkle the salt and granulated garlic over the salmon.

Place the lid on the Instant Pot, making sure the steam-release valve is sealed. Press the Manual button, and set the Instant Pot for 4 minutes.

When the Instant Pot beeps, press Keep Warm/Cancel. Using an oven mitt, "quick release" the steam-release valve. When the steam stops venting and the silver dial drops, carefully open the lid.

Using oven mitts, carefully remove the trivet with the salmon on it from the Instant Pot. Set the trivet on a plate and check the salmon for doneness. If you prefer a crispier salmon, carefully place the salmon on a medium baking sheet and place it under a preheated broiler for 1 to 2 minutes, just until lightly browned, watching closely to prevent burning. Discard the cooking liquid, scallions and crushed garlic.

Finely chop the remaining two scallions, using the white and light green parts only.

Top the hot salmon with the remaining 1 tablespoon (15 g) butter, evenly distributing the butter as it melts. Garnish the salmon with the chopped scallions and parsley, if using. Serve immediately.

NOTES: Avocado oil or ghee can be used as a substitute for the butter if needed. If your salmon fillet is thicker in some areas, you may need to increase the cook time by 1 minute.

SUGAR-FREE RASPBERRY PORK LOIN

PREP TIME: 25 MINUTES
COOK TIME: 51 MINUTES
TOTAL TIME: 76 MINUTES
YIELD: 4 SERVINGS

This tender pork loin infused with aromatic herbs is quite delicious sliced with homemade raspberry sauce slathered on top. The Instant Pot helps cook the meat quickly and perfectly, making this fancier dinner an easy weeknight meal.

3 tbsp (45 g) grass-fed butter or ghee or 3 tbsp (45 ml) avocado oil

1 (1½-lb [680-g]) pork loin

5 cloves garlic, finely chopped

1 tsp fresh thyme leaves

1 tsp finely chopped fresh tarragon

½ tsp finely chopped fresh rosemary

½ cup (120 ml) chicken broth

½ cup (120 ml) dry red wine

1 tbsp (15 ml) apple cider vinegar

1½ tsp (8 g) sea salt

2 cups (250 g) fresh or frozen raspberries

2 tbsp (32 g) granulated erythritol

Add the butter to the Instant Pot and press Sauté. Once the butter has melted, add the pork loin and brown for about 3½ minutes per side. Transfer the pork loin to a plate and set aside.

Add the garlic, thyme, tarragon and rosemary to the Instant Pot and sauté for 2 minutes, stirring occasionally, until fragrant. Add the chicken broth, wine, vinegar and salt, stirring and scraping up any browned bits with a wooden spoon. Press the Keep Warm/Cancel button.

Place the browned pork loin in the Instant Pot. Place the lid on the Instant Pot, making sure the steam-release valve is sealed. Press the Manual button and set the Instant Pot for 25 minutes.

When the Instant Pot beeps, press Keep Warm/Cancel. Allow the Instant Pot to release its pressure naturally for 15 minutes. Using an oven mitt, open the steam-release valve. If there is any steam left over, allow it to release until the silver dial drops, then carefully open the lid.

Carefully remove the pork loin, place it on a large plate and allow it to rest for 5 minutes to help retain the juices.

While the pork loin is resting, place raspberries and erythritol in a small pot over medium heat and cook, stirring occasionally, for about 10 minutes or just until the raspberries break down and become a thick sauce.

Once the pork loin has rested, slice the meat on a bias about ¾ inch (19 mm) thick. Serve the pork immediately with the raspberry sauce poured over the top.

NOTE: Keep the size of your Instant Pot in mind when purchasing the pork loin.

HEARTY ITALIAN-STYLE SAUSAGE AND SWEET PEPPERS

PREP TIME: **20 MINUTES**
COOK TIME: **13 MINUTES**
TOTAL TIME: **33 MINUTES**
YIELD: **4 SERVINGS**

Sausage and peppers make such a fun meal. There's something so simple, primal and comforting about it. This meal cooks quickly in the Instant Pot and is delicious served on its own, over a salad, on top of Low-Carb Turnip and Celery Root Mash (page 133), in lettuce wraps or loaded into your favorite low-carb wraps.

3 tbsp (45 g) grass-fed butter or ghee or 3 tbsp (45 ml) avocado oil

4 to 5 sweet Italian sausages, cut into thick slices on a bias

½ small onion, thickly sliced

3 cloves garlic, finely chopped

2 large bell peppers (any color), tops and seeds removed, thickly sliced

½ cup (120 ml) chicken broth

¾ tsp sea salt

1 tsp dried parsley

1 tsp dried basil

½ tsp dried thyme

½ tsp smoked paprika

Add the butter to the Instant Pot and press Sauté. Once the butter has melted, add the sausages and onion and sauté for 7 minutes, stirring occasionally, until the sausages are browned on the sides. Add the garlic and sauté for 2 minutes, stirring occasionally. Press Keep Warm/Cancel.

Add the bell peppers, chicken broth, salt, parsley, basil, thyme and smoked paprika to the Instant Pot. Stir to combine.

Place the lid on the Instant Pot, making sure the steam-release valve is sealed. Press the Manual button and set the Instant Pot for 4 minutes.

When the Instant Pot beeps, press Keep Warm/Cancel. Allow the Instant Pot to release its pressure naturally for 5 minutes. Using an oven mitt, open the steam-release valve. If there is any steam left over, allow it to release until the silver dial drops, then carefully open the lid.

Use a slotted spoon to scoop out the sausage and peppers and serve immediately.

NOTE: For a fancy twist, garnish the sausage and peppers with a generous amount of freshly grated Parmesan.

BUTTER LOVERS' LEMON-DILL SCALLOPS

PREP TIME: 20 MINUTES
COOK TIME: 5 MINUTES
TOTAL TIME: 25 MINUTES
YIELD: 2 SERVINGS

Scallops are an extra special treat when paired with melted butter infused with lemon and dill. This delicious meal comes together quickly with the Instant Pot's help.

2 tbsp (30 g) ghee or 2 tbsp (30 ml) avocado oil

3 cloves garlic, minced

10 jumbo scallops

1 cup (240 ml) filtered water

½ tsp sea salt

4 tbsp (60 g) grass-fed butter

Juice of 1 lemon

3 tbsp (15 g) finely chopped fresh dill

Add the ghee to the Instant Pot and press Sauté. Once the ghee has melted, add the garlic and sauté for 1 minute. Add the scallops and brown them on each side, about 1 minute per side. Transfer the browned scallops to a plate and set aside. Press Keep Warm/Cancel.

Add the water to the Instant Pot. Place the Instant Pot trivet or steamer basket inside the pot so it's sitting above the water. Place the scallops on top of the trivet or steamer basket and sprinkle the tops of the scallops with the salt.

Place the lid on the Instant Pot, making sure the steam-release valve is sealed. Press the Manual button and set the Instant Pot for 2 minutes.

When the Instant Pot beeps, press Keep Warm/Cancel. Using an oven mitt, "quick release" the steam-release valve. When the steam stops venting and the silver dial drops, carefully open the lid.

Using tongs, carefully transfer the scallops to a serving plate.

In a small pot over medium heat, combine the butter, lemon juice and dill, stirring just until the butter has melted.

Serve the scallops immediately with the lemon-dill butter, either as a dipping sauce, drizzled on the serving plate or on top of the scallops.

HEALTHY ALASKAN COD WITH TOMATO-OLIVE TAPENADE

PREP TIME: **20 MINUTES**
COOK TIME: **4 MINUTES**
TOTAL TIME: **24 MINUTES**
YIELD: **2 SERVINGS**

This salty tomato-olive tapenade is so heavenly paired with the simple steamed whitefish. It's a meal that is easy to make any night of the week, because it cooks so quickly in the Instant Pot—the whole meal is ready in under thirty minutes!

TOMATO-OLIVE TAPENADE

½ cup (88 g) pitted green olives

½ cup (88 g) pitted marinated black olives

7 sun-dried tomatoes packed in olive oil

¼ cup (60 ml) extra virgin olive oil

2 tbsp (10 g) finely chopped fresh Italian parsley

1 clove garlic, crushed

2 tbsp (30 ml) fresh lemon juice

1 oz (28 g) Parmesan cheese, cut into chunks

¼ tsp sea salt

COD

1 cup (240 ml) filtered water

5 cloves garlic, crushed

1 (1-lb [454-g]) wild-caught, skin-on cod fillet

2 tbsp (30 g) grass-fed butter, divided

¾ tsp sea salt

1 tsp granulated garlic

Combine the green olives, black olives, sun-dried tomatoes, oil, parsley, garlic, lemon juice, Parmesan cheese and salt in a food processor. Pulse until everything is roughly chopped and combined, but not fully pureed. Taste for the desired saltiness and add more salt if needed. Store the tapenade in the refrigerator until ready to use.

Add the water and crushed garlic to the Instant Pot. Place the Instant Pot trivet inside the pot so it's sitting above the water.

Place the cod, skin side down, on top of the trivet. Place 1 tablespoon (15 g) of the butter on top of the cod. Sprinkle the salt and granulated garlic over the cod.

Place the lid on the Instant Pot, making sure the steam-release valve is sealed. Press the Manual button and set the Instant Pot for 4 minutes.

When the Instant Pot beeps, press Keep Warm/Cancel. Using an oven mitt, "quick release" the steam-release valve. When the steam stops venting and the silver dial drops, carefully open the lid.

Using oven mitts, carefully remove the trivet with the cod on it from the Instant Pot. Set the trivet on a plate and check the cod for doneness. If you prefer a crispier cod, carefully place the cod on a medium baking sheet and place it under a preheated broiler for 1 to 2 minutes, just until lightly browned, watching closely to prevent burning. Discard the cooking liquid and crushed garlic.

Top the hot cod with the remaining tablespoon (15 g) of butter, evenly distributing the butter as it melts. Garnish the cod with the tomato-olive tapenade. Serve immediately.

NOTES: If the fish is too large for your Instant Pot, it can be cut in half and set side-by-side on the trivet. Avocado oil or ghee can be used as a substitute for the butter if needed. If your cod fillet is thicker in some areas, you may need to increase the cook time by 1 minute. If it is very thin, decrease the cook time by 1 minute.

STEAMED BUTTERY GARLIC-HERB CLAMS

PREP TIME: **20 MINUTES**
COOK TIME: **7 MINUTES**
TOTAL TIME: **27 MINUTES**
YIELD: **10+ SERVINGS**

You can't get much simpler than steamed clams. They're one of the easiest things to make in the Instant Pot and can serve a crowd if needed. These delicious clams cook in a bath of melted butter, dry white wine, lemon juice and fresh herbs.

5 tbsp (75 g) grass-fed butter

5 cloves garlic, minced

½ tsp sea salt

Juice of 1 lemon

¼ cup (15 g) finely chopped fresh Italian parsley, plus more if desired

3 fresh thyme sprigs, plus more if desired

1 tbsp (5 g) finely chopped fresh tarragon, plus more if desired

1 cup (240 ml) dry white wine

3 lb (1.4 kg) fresh clams, cleaned and scrubbed

Lemon wedges (optional)

Add the butter to the Instant Pot and press Sauté. Once the butter has melted, add the garlic and sauté for 2 minutes. Add the salt, lemon juice, parsley, thyme, tarragon and wine and cook until the mixture comes to a boil, about 1 minute. Press Keep Warm/Cancel. Carefully add the clams to the Instant Pot.

Place the lid on the Instant Pot, making sure the steam-release valve is sealed. Press the Manual button, and set the Instant Pot for 4 minutes.

When the Instant Pot beeps, press Keep Warm/Cancel. Using an oven mitt, "quick release" the steam-release valve. When the steam stops venting and the silver dial drops, carefully open the lid.

Using tongs, discard any clams that did not open, as they will not be safe to eat. Carefully transfer the clams and cooking liquid to a serving bowl.

Serve the clams as they are or garnished with additional parsley, thyme, tarragon and lemon wedges, if desired.

NOTE: Fresh mint can be substituted for the tarragon if needed.

CITRUS-HERB GAME HEN

PREP TIME: **25 MINUTES**
COOK TIME: **19 MINUTES**
TOTAL TIME: **44 MINUTES**
YIELD: **2 TO 4 SERVINGS**

While Cornish game hen seems like a fancy meal, it certainly does not take a long time to make when you cook it in the Instant Pot. This poultry takes fewer than thirty minutes to cook, leaving you plenty of time to fix a delicious side to go with it, like homemade low-carb gravy and Low-Carb Turnip and Celery Root Mash (page 133).

1 tsp sea salt

Zest of 1 orange

Zest of 1 lemon

¼ cup (15 g) finely chopped fresh Italian parsley, plus more as needed

1 tbsp (3 g) fresh thyme leaves

2 tsp (1 g) finely chopped fresh rosemary

2 tsp (2 g) dried dill

1 (2-lb [908-g]) Cornish game hen

6 tbsp (90 g) grass-fed butter or ghee, melted, divided

½ cup (120 ml) dry white wine

¼ cup (60 ml) freshly squeezed orange juice

¼ cup (60 ml) freshly squeezed lemon juice

Orange and lemon slices (optional)

In a small bowl, combine the salt, orange zest, lemon zest, parsley, thyme, rosemary and dill, stirring to combine. Set aside.

Place the game hen on a large plate. Rub 4 tablespoons (60 g) of the butter on the skin and underneath the skin of the game hen. Evenly distribute and rub the salt-zest-herb seasoning all over the skin, underneath the skin and inside the cavity. Set the game hen aside and wash your hands.

Add the remaining 2 tablespoons (30 g) butter to the Instant Pot and press Sauté. Once the butter has melted, add the game hen, breast-side down, browning the skin for 3 minutes. Flip and brown the other side for 3 minutes. Add the white wine, orange juice and lemon juice and flip the game hen with tongs so it's breast-side up. Press Keep Warm/Cancel.

Place the lid on the Instant Pot, making sure the steam-release valve is sealed. Press the Manual button and set the Instant Pot for 13 minutes.

When the Instant Pot beeps, press Keep Warm/Cancel. Allow the Instant Pot to release its pressure naturally for 15 minutes. Using an oven mitt, open the steam-release valve. If there is any steam left over, allow it to release until the silver dial drops, then carefully open the lid.

Use a meat thermometer to confirm that the internal temperature of the game hen is 165°F (74°C). If it's not, press Manual and cook for 2 minutes, then use a quick pressure release.

Serve the game hen immediately, garnished with optional citrus slices, if desired, and additional parsley.

NOTE: If you prefer a crispier skin, you can place the cooked game hen on a medium baking sheet under a preheated broiler for 2 to 4 minutes, just until lightly golden brown. Do not walk away or it will burn!

SPINACH AND CHEESE-STUFFED CHICKEN BREASTS

PREP TIME: 25 MINUTES
COOK TIME: 10 MINUTES
TOTAL TIME: 35 MINUTES
YIELD: 2 SERVINGS

We love the convenience of dinners that provide both protein and veggies in the same meal. These stuffed chicken breasts fit the bill: Each butterflied chicken breast gets stuffed with a delicious mixture of spinach, cheddar, Parmesan and feta cheeses, parsley and dill and a hint of zesty lemon.

2 (4-oz [112-g]) boneless and skinless chicken breasts

1 cup (156 g) frozen chopped spinach, thawed and moisture squeezed out

½ cup (120 g) cream cheese, softened

½ cup (60 g) shredded cheddar cheese

¼ cup (25 g) shredded Parmesan cheese

¼ cup (38 g) crumbled feta cheese

1 tsp sea salt

1 tsp granulated garlic or garlic powder

1 tsp dried dill

Zest of 1 lemon

¼ cup (15 g) finely chopped fresh Italian parsley, plus more as needed

1 cup (240 ml) filtered water

2 tbsp (30 ml) melted butter or ghee or avocado oil, divided

6 thin lemon slices, divided

On a cutting board with a sharp knife, carefully butterfly both chicken breasts by slicing them lengthwise down the center of the breasts until you've almost cut through the whole chicken breast. Fan the breasts open. Set aside.

In a mixing bowl, combine the spinach, cream cheese, cheddar cheese, Parmesan cheese, feta cheese, salt, granulated garlic, dill, lemon zest and parsley and gently mix until everything is fully distributed. Add half of the filling to the bottom side of each of the fanned-open chicken breasts. Then carefully fold the tops of the chicken breasts over the filling. Secure each chicken breast with a toothpick.

Place the Instant Pot trivet inside the Instant Pot. Pour the water into the Instant Pot. Carefully transfer the stuffed chicken breasts to the Instant Pot on top of the trivet. Drizzle each chicken breast with 1 tablespoon (15 ml) of the butter. Top each chicken breast with 3 lemon slices.

Place the lid on the Instant Pot, making sure the steam-release valve is sealed. Press the Manual button and set the Instant Pot for 10 minutes.

When the Instant Pot beeps, press Keep Warm/Cancel. Allow the Instant Pot to release its pressure naturally for 15 minutes. Using an oven mitt, open the steam-release valve. If there is any steam left over, allow it to release until the silver dial drops, then carefully open the lid.

Carefully remove the trivet with the chicken breasts from the Instant Pot.

Serve immediately garnished with additional parsley, if desired.

HIGH-FAT SHRIMP SCAMPI

PREP TIME: **15 MINUTES**
COOK TIME: **3 MINUTES**
TOTAL TIME: **18 MINUTES**
YIELD: **4 SERVINGS**

Who doesn't love shrimp scampi? Garlic, salt and butter—need I say more? You can't go wrong with those little meaty bites doused in simple ingredients. Set the table quickly, because these tasty crustaceans are done in just a few minutes.

4 tbsp (60 g) grass-fed butter

5 cloves garlic, minced

¼ cup (60 ml) fresh lemon juice

½ cup (120 ml) dry white wine

¼ cup (60 ml) chicken broth

2 lb (908 g) large shrimp, peeled and deveined

1 tsp sea salt

¼ cup (15 g) finely chopped fresh Italian parsley

Add the butter to the Instant Pot and press Sauté. Once the butter has melted, add the garlic and sauté for 1 minute, stirring occasionally. Add the lemon juice, wine, chicken broth, shrimp and salt and stir. Press Keep Warm/Cancel.

Place the lid on the Instant Pot, making sure the steam-release valve is sealed. Press the Manual button and set the Instant Pot for 2 minutes.

When the Instant Pot beeps, press Keep Warm/Cancel. Using an oven mitt, "quick release" the steam-release valve. When the steam stops venting and the silver dial drops, carefully open the lid.

Transfer the shrimp to a large serving plate and top them with the parsley. Serve immediately.

NOTE: For the most authentic scampi taste, use butter. Ghee or avocado oil can be used as a substitute for the butter if needed.

SIMPLE CASSEROLES AND DELICIOUS QUICHES

Kiss store-bought packaged foods goodbye. No longer will you have to make frozen or boxed casseroles—now you can enjoy delicious meals at the press of a button without frostbite or unnatural preservatives.

Indulge in a bowl of Southern-Style Cheesy Shrimp Casserole (page 79) or savor our Cauliflower Pizza Casserole (page 72). Either way, you can't lose!

For our low-carb take on more traditional recipes, try the Broccoli-Cauliflower Mac and Cheese Casserole (page 76) or the Crustless Veggie and Bacon Quiche (page 75).

Enjoy the coziness of these easy-to-prepare, grain-free recipes and eat to your heart's content.

CAULIFLOWER PIZZA CASSEROLE

PREP TIME: **25 MINUTES**
COOK TIME: **16 MINUTES**
TOTAL TIME: **41 MINUTES**
YIELD: **4 TO 6 SERVINGS**

You can still enjoy the flavors of cheesy pepperoni, mushroom and olive "pizza" on a low-carb diet—in casserole form. This cauliflower-based casserole is packed with a hefty dose of veggies, and the zesty Italian seasoning that goes into pizza sauce. The best part is it cooks very quickly in the Instant Pot, so you'll be enjoying "pizza night" in no time.

½ cup (120 ml) crushed tomatoes

½ cup (120 g) cream cheese, softened

1 cup (111 g) shredded mozzarella cheese

¾ cup (75 g) shredded Parmesan cheese

1 large head cauliflower, cut into bite-size florets

1 tsp sea salt

1½ tsp (5 g) granulated garlic granules or garlic powder

½ tsp onion powder

¼ cup (15 g) finely chopped fresh Italian parsley, plus more as needed

½ tsp dried thyme

½ tsp dried oregano

¼ tsp freshly ground black pepper

1 cup (70 g) thickly sliced mushrooms

½ cup (90 g) thickly sliced black olives

2 oz (56 g) sliced pepperoni

1 cup (240 ml) filtered water

Grease a 1½-quart (1.5-L) baking dish with a glass lid that fits in the Instant Pot. Set aside.

In a large bowl, combine the crushed tomatoes, cream cheese, mozzarella cheese, Parmesan cheese, cauliflower, salt, granulated garlic, onion powder, parsley, thyme, oregano, pepper, mushrooms and olives and gently mix until everything is incorporated. Add the filling to the baking dish. In a uniform layer, line the pepperoni on top of the casserole filling. Place the glass lid on top of the baking dish.

Place the Instant Pot trivet inside the Instant Pot. Pour the water into the Instant Pot. Carefully transfer the covered baking dish to the Instant Pot on top of the trivet.

Place the lid on the Instant Pot, making sure the steam-release valve is sealed. Press the Manual button and set the Instant Pot for 13 minutes.

When the Instant Pot beeps, press Keep Warm/Cancel. Allow the Instant Pot to release its pressure naturally for 15 minutes. Using an oven mitt, open the steam-release valve. If there is any steam left over, allow it to release until the silver dial drops, then carefully open the lid.

While the Instant Pot is releasing its pressure, preheat the oven to broil.

Carefully remove the baking dish from the Instant Pot and remove the lid. Place the baking dish on a medium baking sheet and place under the broiler for 2 to 3 minutes, just until the pepperoni becomes light golden brown or crispy around the edges. Serve immediately garnished with additional parsley.

NOTES: If you don't have a lid for your baking dish, you can place a piece of parchment paper over the top then cover it securely with foil.

Quality, natural or organic pepperoni brands are very easy to find in natural-foods stores and most grocery stores.

CRUSTLESS VEGGIE AND BACON QUICHE

PREP TIME: 25 MINUTES
COOK TIME: 38 MINUTES
TOTAL TIME: 63 MINUTES
YIELD: 6 SERVINGS

Quiche is one of those foods that can be considered gourmet and comfort food at the same time. This dish cooks perfectly in the Instant Pot and is packed with caramelized mushrooms, nourishing spinach, crispy bacon, several cheeses and a hint of lemon and herbs.

½ cup (50 g) shredded Parmesan cheese, divided

¼ cup (30 g) shredded cheddar cheese, divided

¼ cup (28 g) shredded provolone or Gruyère cheese, divided

2 tbsp (30 g) grass-fed butter or ghee, plus more as needed

1 cup (70 g) thinly sliced or finely chopped mushrooms

2 cups (60 g) prewashed fresh spinach, coarsely chopped

5 large eggs

½ cup (120 ml) heavy cream

¼ cup (60 g) cream cheese, softened

1 tsp sea salt

1 tsp granulated garlic

7 slices crispy cooked bacon, crumbled

Zest of 1 lemon

¼ cup (15 g) finely chopped fresh Italian parsley

1 cup (240 ml) filtered water

In a medium bowl, combine the Parmesan cheese, cheddar cheese and provolone cheese. Set the cheese mixture aside.

Add the butter to the Instant Pot and press Sauté. Once the butter has melted, add the mushrooms and sauté for 7 minutes, stirring occasionally until they are lightly caramelized. Add the spinach and sauté for 3 minutes, stirring occasionally, just until it is wilted. Press the Keep Warm/Cancel button.

Grease a 1½-quart (1.5-L) baking dish with a glass lid that fits inside the Instant Pot. Set it aside.

In a large bowl, whisk together the eggs, heavy cream and cream cheese until the eggs are fully incorporated. Add the salt, granulated garlic, bacon, lemon zest, parsley, three-quarters of the cheese mixture and the mushroom mixture, gently stirring to combine. Pour the mixture into the prepared baking dish. Place the lid on the baking dish.

Pour the water into the Instant Pot. Place the Instant Pot trivet in the Instant Pot. Carefully transfer the covered baking dish into the Instant Pot on top of the trivet. Place the lid on the Instant Pot, making sure the steam-release valve is sealed. Press the Manual button and set the Instant Pot for 25 minutes.

When the Instant Pot beeps, press Keep Warm/Cancel. Allow the Instant Pot to naturally release its pressure for 10 minutes. Using an oven mitt, "quick release" the steam-release valve. When the steam stops venting and the silver dial drops, carefully open the lid.

Carefully remove the baking dish from the Instant Pot and remove the lid from the dish. Next, add the remaining one-quarter of the reserved cheese mixture to the top of the quiche and either place the baking dish back in the Instant Pot, covered with the Instant Pot lid for about 3 minutes to melt the cheese or place it under a preheated broiler in the oven for about 3 minutes, or just until the cheese is lightly browned.

Allow the quiche to rest for 15 minutes before serving.

NOTE: If your baking dish doesn't have a glass lid, you can cover the top of the dish with unbleached parchment paper then top it with foil and secure it around the edges.

BROCCOLI-CAULIFLOWER MAC AND CHEESE CASSEROLE

PREP TIME: 25 MINUTES
COOK TIME: 13 MINUTES
TOTAL TIME: 38 MINUTES
YIELD: 4 TO 6 SERVINGS

We are big-time mac and cheese lovers. In fact, my fondness for it began at a very young age—I even had a friend give me boxes of the store-bought kind at my fourth birthday party! This low-carb version satisfies the mac and cheese craving without the pasta, plus you get the added benefit of eating your veggies at the same time.

1½ cups (180 g) shredded cheddar cheese

¾ cup (75 g) shredded Parmesan cheese

¼ cup (28 g) shredded Gruyère cheese

½ cup (120 g) cream cheese, softened

¼ cup (58 g) sour cream

3½ cups (350 g) riced cauliflower (not frozen)

2 small heads broccoli, cut into bite-size florets

1 tsp sea salt

1 cup (240 ml) filtered water

2 tbsp (10 g) finely chopped fresh Italian parsley (optional)

In a medium bowl, combine the cheddar cheese, Parmesan cheese and Gruyère cheese. Set the cheese mixture aside.

Grease a 1½-quart (1.5-L) baking dish with a glass lid that fits in the Instant Pot. Set aside.

In a large bowl, combine the cream cheese, sour cream, three-quarters of the cheese mixture, riced cauliflower, broccoli and salt and gently mix.

Transfer the mixture to the baking dish, then sprinkle the remaining one-quarter of the reserved cheese mixture over the top. Place the lid on top of the casserole dish. Place the Instant Pot trivet inside the Instant Pot. Pour the water into the Instant Pot. Carefully transfer the covered baking dish to the Instant Pot on top of the trivet.

Place the lid on the Instant Pot, making sure the steam-release valve is sealed. Press the Manual button and set the Instant Pot for 10 minutes.

When the Instant Pot beeps, press Keep Warm/Cancel. Allow the Instant Pot to release its pressure naturally for 15 minutes. Using an oven mitt, open the steam-release valve. If there is any steam left over, allow it to release until the silver dial drops, then carefully open the lid.

While the Instant Pot is releasing its pressure, preheat the oven to broil.

Carefully remove the baking dish from the Instant Pot and remove the lid. Place the casserole dish on a small baking sheet and place it under the broiler for 2 to 3 minutes, just until the top becomes slightly bubbly and the cheese becomes light golden brown. Serve immediately garnished with parsley, if desired.

NOTE: If you don't have a lid for your baking dish, you can place a piece of parchment paper over the top, then cover it securely with foil.

SOUTHERN-STYLE CHEESY SHRIMP CASSEROLE

PREP TIME: **25 MINUTES**
COOK TIME: **7 MINUTES**
TOTAL TIME: **32 MINUTES**
YIELD: **4 TO 6 SERVINGS**

Shrimp, cheesy goodness, okra, celery and hints of classic seafood seasoning—that's what this delicious casserole is about. This shrimp casserole is brimming with three cheeses, lots of veggies and a whole bunch of flavor. It satisfies my Southern roots and my husband's love of shrimp and, oh my goodness, it's so good!

½ cup (120 g) cream cheese, softened

¼ cup (60 ml) heavy cream

1½ cups (180 g) shredded cheddar cheese

½ cup (50 g) shredded Parmesan cheese

2 tbsp (30 g) grass-fed butter or ghee, melted, plus more as needed

1½ lb (680 g) large shrimp, peeled and deveined

½ small green bell pepper, top and seeds removed, diced

2 large celery ribs, cut into ¼-inch (6-mm) thick pieces or diced

5 pods okra, tops and seeds removed, thinly sliced

2 scallions (white parts only), finely chopped

1 cup (100 g) riced cauliflower (not frozen)

1 tsp sea salt

1 tsp granulated garlic or garlic powder

½ tsp onion powder

Zest of 1 lemon

¼ cup (15 g) finely chopped fresh Italian parsley, plus more as needed

½ tsp dried thyme

½ tsp smoked paprika or paprika

¼ tsp ground bay leaf

¼ tsp freshly ground black pepper

1 cup (240 ml) filtered water

Grease a 1½-quart (1.5-L) baking dish with a glass lid that fits in the Instant Pot. Set aside.

In a large bowl, combine the cream cheese, heavy cream, cheddar cheese, Parmesan cheese, butter, shrimp, bell pepper, celery, okra, scallions, cauliflower, salt, granulated garlic, onion powder, lemon zest, parsley, thyme, smoked paprika, bay leaf and black pepper and gently mix. Transfer the mixture to the baking dish. Place the lid on the baking dish.

Place the Instant Pot trivet inside the Instant Pot. Pour the water into the Instant Pot. Carefully transfer the covered baking dish to the Instant Pot on top of the trivet. Place the lid on the Instant Pot, making sure the steam-release valve is sealed. Press the Manual button and set the Instant Pot for 5 minutes.

When the Instant Pot beeps, press Keep Warm/Cancel. Allow the Instant Pot to release its pressure naturally for 15 minutes. Using an oven mitt, open the steam-release valve. If there is any steam left over, allow it to release until the silver dial drops, then carefully open the lid.

While the Instant Pot is releasing its pressure, preheat the oven to broil.

Carefully remove the baking dish from the Instant Pot and remove the lid. Place the baking dish on a small baking sheet and place it under the broiler for 2 minutes, just until the top becomes bubbly and light golden brown. Serve immediately, garnished with additional parsley.

NOTE: If you don't have a lid for your baking dish, you can place a piece of parchment paper over the top, then cover it securely with foil.

CRUSTLESS GREEK VEGGIE QUICHE

PREP TIME: 25 MINUTES
COOK TIME: 28 MINUTES
TOTAL TIME: 53 MINUTES
YIELD: 6 SERVINGS

We're big crustless-quiche fans in our home. We find crustless quiche is a great way to get a serving of protein and healthy fats—plus you can pack it with lots of good-for-you ingredients like veggies. We love making this Greek veggie quiche and serving it for breakfast, lunch or dinner. It's perfect for any meal of the day!

5 large eggs

½ cup (120 ml) heavy cream

½ cup (120 g) cream cheese, softened

1 tsp sea salt

1 tsp granulated garlic

Zest of 1 lemon

1 small tomato, seeds removed, coarsely chopped

1 cup (156 g) frozen chopped spinach, thawed and moisture squeezed out

1 small red bell pepper, stem and seeds removed, diced

½ cup (90 g) Kalamata olives, halved

½ cup (30 g) finely chopped fresh Italian parsley

¼ cup (15 g) finely chopped fresh mint

1 cup (100 g) shredded Parmesan cheese, divided

¼ cup (28 g) shredded provolone or Gruyère cheese

¼ cup (38 g) crumbled feta cheese

1 cup (240 ml) filtered water

Grease a 1½-quart (1.5-L) baking dish (with a glass lid) that fits inside the Instant Pot. Set it aside.

In a large bowl, whisk together the eggs, heavy cream and cream cheese until the eggs are fully incorporated. Add the salt, granulated garlic, lemon zest, tomato, spinach, bell pepper, olives, parsley, mint, ¾ cup (75 g) of the Parmesan cheese, provolone cheese and feta cheese and gently mix. Transfer the mixture to the prepared baking dish. Place the lid on the baking dish.

Pour the water into the Instant Pot. Place the Instant Pot trivet in the Instant Pot. Carefully transfer the covered baking dish into the Instant Pot on top of the trivet.

Place the lid on the Instant Pot, making sure the steam-release valve is sealed. Press the Manual button and set the Instant Pot for 25 minutes.

When the Instant Pot beeps, press Keep Warm/Cancel. Allow the Instant Pot to naturally release its pressure for 10 minutes. Using an oven mitt, "quick release" the steam-release valve. When the steam stops venting and the silver dial drops, carefully open the lid.

Carefully remove the baking dish from the Instant Pot and remove the lid from the dish. Add the remaining ¼ cup (25 g) Parmesan cheese to the top of the quiche and either place the dish back in the Instant Pot, covered with the Instant Pot lid, for about 3 minutes to melt the cheese or place it under a preheated broiler in the oven for about 3 minutes, or just until the cheese is lightly browned.

Allow the quiche to rest for 15 minutes before serving.

NOTE: If your casserole dish doesn't have a glass lid, you can cover the top of the dish with unbleached parchment paper then top it with foil and secure it around the edges.

EASY-PEASY SOUPS AND STEWS

You don't need to wait all day by your stovetop or slow cooker for your favorite soups and hearty stews to simmer and be perfectly cooked. You can get the same tender, juicy morsels of stew meat, delectable seafood bisques and flavor-packed soups in just minutes using your Instant Pot!

No longer will you have to heat up processed soups and stews from BPA-laden cans. Now you can have delicious and nutritious meals with just the press of a button.

Enjoy a warm bowl of Healthier Broccoli-Cheese Soup (page 86), take a quick getaway to the coast within the comforts of your own home with Nourishing Crab Bisque (page 118) or get cozy and dunk your spoon in a piping hot bowl of Italian Wedding Soup (page 126).

These recipes were made to be easy-peasy and sure-to-pleasy, so whatever you decide to make, it's a win!

HEARTY CLAM CHOWDER

PREP TIME: 20 MINUTES
COOK TIME: 8 MINUTES
TOTAL TIME: 28 MINUTES
YIELD: 4 TO 6 SERVINGS

My husband and I have a fondness for clam chowder. It's one of the spur-of-the-moment foods that we had at our wedding in Bodega Bay, California. Ever since then, we've enjoyed re-creating our own version of this dish as a celebration on our anniversary and other special occasions. This delectable, low-carb version is so yummy, you won't even miss the potatoes or flour-based roux.

3 tbsp (45 g) grass-fed butter

1 medium shallot, diced

4 cloves garlic, finely chopped

3 large celery ribs, cut into ¼-inch (6-mm) thick pieces

2 cups (214 g) cauliflower florets, finely chopped

¼ cup (15 g) finely chopped Italian parsley

1½ cups (360 ml) clam juice

½ cup (120 ml) fish stock, chicken broth or vegetable broth

1 tsp sea salt

½ tsp freshly ground black pepper

2 tsp (2 g) fresh thyme leaves

Zest of 1 lemon

13 oz (364 g) canned clams, drained

2 cups (480 ml) heavy cream

1 cup (240 g) cream cheese

1 tbsp (3 g) finely chopped chives

Add the butter to the Instant Pot and press Sauté. Once the butter has melted, add the shallot and sauté for 4 minutes, stirring occasionally. Add the garlic and sauté for 1 minute, stirring occasionally. Press Keep Warm/Cancel.

Add the celery, cauliflower, parsley, clam juice, fish stock, salt, black pepper, thyme, lemon zest and clams to the Instant Pot. Stir to combine.

Place the lid on the Instant Pot, making sure the steam-release valve is sealed. Press the Manual button and set the Instant Pot for 3 minutes.

When the Instant Pot beeps, press Keep Warm/Cancel. Using an oven mitt, "quick release" the steam-release valve. When the steam stops venting and the silver dial drops, carefully open the lid.

Add the heavy cream, cream cheese and chives, then stir until the cream cheese is fully mixed in. Taste it to check the seasoning, and add more salt if you prefer it saltier.

Serve immediately.

NOTE: Try to find sustainable canned clams. Usually, you can find them in larger natural-foods stores or online. Otherwise, look for BPA-free cans of clams or clam juice that come in glass jars.

HEALTHIER BROCCOLI-CHEESE SOUP

PREP TIME: 15 MINUTES
COOK TIME: 6 MINUTES
TOTAL TIME: 21 MINUTES
YIELD: 4 TO 6 SERVINGS

Skip the chain restaurant and get the comfort of broccoli cheese soup right at home! Grab a bowl and some shredded cheese, because the Instant Pot will have your soup made in minutes.

3 tbsp (45 g) grass-fed butter

5 cloves garlic, minced

4 cups (624 g) fresh or frozen broccoli florets

2 cups (480 ml) chicken or vegetable broth

1 tsp sea salt

1 tsp celery flakes

½ tsp dried dill

2½ cups (300 g) shredded cheddar cheese, plus more as needed (see Note)

1½ cups (360 ml) heavy cream

Add the butter to the Instant Pot and press Sauté. Once the butter has melted, add the garlic and sauté for 1 minute, stirring occasionally. Add the broccoli, broth, salt, celery flakes and dill. Stir to combine. Press Keep Warm/Cancel.

Place the lid on the Instant Pot, making sure the steam-release valve is sealed. Press the Manual button and set the Instant Pot for 5 minutes.

When the Instant Pot beeps, press Keep Warm/Cancel. Allow the Instant Pot to release its pressure naturally for 5 minutes. Using an oven mitt, open the steam-release valve. If there is any steam left over, allow it to release until the silver dial drops, then carefully open the lid.

Add the cheddar cheese and stir immediately until the cheese is incorporated, then add the cream and continue to stir until it's mixed in.

Measure out 1 cup (240 ml) of soup and set aside. Carefully pour the remaining soup into a high-powered blender or leave it in the Instant Pot and use an immersion blender, leaving at least 3 inches (8 cm) of space from the top of the blender. Blend on low speed just until the soup is homogenous, about 5 seconds. Pour the soup back into the Instant Pot. Add the reserved 1 cup (240 ml) of soup and stir.

Taste the soup for seasoning and add more salt if you prefer it saltier. Serve immediately, garnished with additional cheddar cheese.

NOTE: Using store-bought shredded cheese works best for this soup and helps prevent lumpy cheese that doesn't mix as well. A fifty-fifty mix of cheddar cheese and Monterey Jack cheese can be used instead of all cheddar.

CREAM OF ASPARAGUS SOUP

PREP TIME: 20 MINUTES
COOK TIME: 5 MINUTES
TOTAL TIME: 25 MINUTES
YIELD: 4 TO 6 SERVINGS

We make Cream of Asparagus Soup often during the spring, when asparagus is growing like crazy. We love to liven this delicious soup up with fresh herbs and a hint of tangy lemon, flavors that go perfectly with the creamy asparagus base.

3 tbsp (45 g) grass-fed butter

2 lb (908 g) fresh asparagus, cut into thirds, woody ends removed

¼ cup (15 g) finely chopped fresh Italian parsley

4 cups (960 ml) chicken or vegetable broth

1 tsp sea salt

1 tsp granulated garlic

½ tsp dried thyme

½ tsp dried dill

Zest of 1 lemon

1 cup (240 ml) heavy cream

1 cup (230 g) sour cream, plus more as needed

Shredded Parmesan cheese (optional)

Freshly ground black pepper (optional)

Add the butter, asparagus, parsley, chicken broth, salt, granulated garlic, thyme, dill and lemon zest to the Instant Pot. Stir to combine.

Place the lid on the Instant Pot, making sure the steam-release valve is sealed. Press the Manual button and set the Instant Pot for 5 minutes.

When the Instant Pot beeps, press Keep Warm/Cancel. Allow the Instant Pot to release its pressure naturally for 5 minutes. Using an oven mitt, open the steam-release valve. If there is any steam left over, allow it to release until the silver dial drops, then carefully open the lid.

Add the heavy cream and sour cream, stirring to combine.

Carefully pour the soup into a high-powered blender or leave it in the Instant Pot and use an immersion blender, leaving at least 3 inches (8 cm) of space from the top of the blender, then blend on low speed just until the soup is homogenous, about 5 seconds. You may need to do this in batches.

Taste the soup for seasoning and add more salt if you prefer it saltier. Transfer the soup to the Instant Pot. Press Sauté, bring the soup to a boil and stir a few times. Press Keep Warm/Cancel.

Serve the soup immediately as is or topped with a dollop of additional sour cream. It's also delicious sprinkled with a little shredded Parmesan cheese and freshly ground black pepper, if desired.

NOTE: Two pounds (908 g) of asparagus is approximately two bunches of asparagus.

PERFECT REPLICA FRENCH ONION SOUP

PREP TIME: 20 MINUTES
COOK TIME: 21 MINUTES
TOTAL TIME: 41 MINUTES
YIELD: 4 TO 6 SERVINGS

Oh French onion soup, how I love you! When I was a little girl, my mom would take me to this little French café, and we'd always get a cup of French onion soup to go with our meal. It was so special and so good, and ever since then it's been a favorite. Luckily, my husband loves it too. We enjoy prepping this grain-free version together and then letting the Instant Pot cook it for us.

4 tbsp (60 g) grass-fed butter or ghee

2 large yellow onions, thickly sliced

4 scallions (white and light green parts only), thinly sliced

5 cloves garlic, finely chopped

½ cup (120 ml) dry white wine

4 cups (960 ml) beef or chicken broth

1 tbsp (15 ml) apple cider vinegar

1 tsp sea salt

2 tsp (2 g) fresh thyme leaves

2 fresh or dried bay leaves

⅛ tsp freshly ground black pepper

1 cup (112 g) shredded Gruyère cheese

¼ cup (25 g) shredded Parmesan cheese

Add the butter to the Instant Pot and press Sauté. Once the butter has melted, add the onions and scallions and sauté for 15 minutes, stirring occasionally until the onions turn golden brown and begin to caramelize. Add the garlic, stir and sauté for 1 minute. Add the wine to deglaze the pot, scraping up any browned bits with a wooden spoon. Press Keep Warm/Cancel.

Add the broth, vinegar, salt, thyme, bay leaves and black pepper to the Instant Pot. Stir to combine.

Place the lid on the Instant Pot, making sure the steam-release valve is sealed. Press the Manual button, and set the Instant Pot for 3 minutes.

When the Instant Pot beeps, press Keep Warm/Cancel. Using an oven mitt, "quick release" the steam-release valve. When the steam stops venting and the silver dial drops, carefully open the lid. With tongs or a spoon, remove and discard the bay leaves.

Taste the soup for seasoning, and add more salt if you prefer it saltier.

Preheat the oven to broil.

Ladle the soup into broiler-safe bowls and place the bowls on a large baking sheet. Evenly sprinkle the Gruyère cheese and Parmesan cheese over the top of the soup. Carefully place the soup under the broiler for 1 to 2 minutes, just until the cheese gets bubbly and slightly golden brown in some areas.

Serve the soup immediately.

NOTE: If you don't want to broil the cheese, you can skip this step. The cheese will still melt over the hot soup and be just as yummy.

CREAMY TOMATO BISQUE

PREP TIME: 20 MINUTES
COOK TIME: 6 MINUTES
TOTAL TIME: 26 MINUTES
YIELD: 4 TO 6 SERVINGS

Tomato bisque holds a special place in my heart. When I was a teenager, my grandma used to take me to a little tea house called The Camellia Tea Room. We would get the traditional tea service, which consisted of tea sandwiches, scones, small treats and tea, and we always added a cup of their tomato bisque. This Instant Pot version is in honor of my grandma.

3 tbsp (45 g) grass-fed butter

5 cloves garlic, finely chopped

4 cups (960 ml) crushed tomatoes

1 small bulb fennel, tough outer stalks removed, cored and sliced

¼ cup (15 g) finely chopped fresh basil, plus more as needed

¼ cup (15 g) finely chopped fresh Italian parsley

3 cups (720 ml) chicken or vegetable broth

1 tsp sea salt

½ tsp dried thyme

¼ tsp onion powder

Zest of 1 lemon

¼ cup (60 g) mascarpone cheese or cream cheese, plus more as needed

1 cup (240 ml) heavy cream

Freshly ground black pepper (optional)

Extra virgin olive oil (optional)

Add the butter to the Instant Pot and press Sauté. Once the butter has melted, add the garlic and sauté for 1 minute, stirring occasionally. Press Keep Warm/Cancel.

Add the crushed tomatoes, fennel, basil, parsley, broth, salt, thyme, onion powder and lemon zest to the Instant Pot. Stir to combine.

Place the lid on the Instant Pot, making sure the steam-release valve is sealed. Press the Manual button, and set the Instant Pot for 5 minutes.

When the Instant Pot beeps, press Keep Warm/Cancel. Allow the Instant Pot to release its pressure naturally for 5 minutes. Using an oven mitt, open the steam-release valve. If there is any steam left over, allow it to release until the silver dial drops, then carefully open the lid.

Add the mascarpone cheese, stirring until it's mixed in.

Carefully pour the soup into a high-powered blender or it leave in the Instant Pot and use an immersion blender, leaving at least 3 inches (8 cm) of space from the top of the blender, then blend on low speed just until the soup is homogenous, about 5 seconds. You may need to do this in batches.

Taste the soup for seasoning and add more salt if you prefer it saltier. Transfer the soup to the Instant Pot. Press Sauté, bring the soup to a boil and stir a few times. Add the heavy cream, stirring until incorporated, then press Keep Warm/Cancel.

Serve immediately as is or topped with a dollop of mascarpone or freshly chopped basil. Alternatively, it's also delicious sprinkled with freshly ground black pepper and a drizzle of extra virgin olive oil, if desired.

JALAPEÑO, BACON AND CHEDDAR SOUP

PREP TIME: 15 MINUTES
COOK TIME: 5 MINUTES
TOTAL TIME: 20 MINUTES
YIELD: 4 TO 6 SERVINGS

Jalapeños, bacon and cheddar are a match made in heaven. Best friends or triplets, these three are meant to be together and do so perfectly in this pureed soup. If you enjoy a spicy kick, you're going to love this hearty soup.

3 tbsp (45 g) grass-fed butter

3 cups (321 g) fresh or frozen cauliflower florets

2 large or 4 small jalapeños, stems and seeds removed, finely chopped

3 cups (720 ml) chicken or vegetable broth

1 tsp sea salt

1 tsp granulated garlic

½ tsp dried thyme

½ tsp ground cumin

¼ tsp dried oregano

2 cups (240 g) shredded cheddar cheese, plus more as needed

2 cups (480 ml) heavy cream

½ cup (115 g) sour cream

7 slices crispy cooked bacon, crumbled

Thinly sliced jalapeños (optional)

Add the butter, cauliflower, jalapeños, broth, salt, granulated garlic, thyme, cumin and oregano to the Instant Pot. Stir to combine.

Place the lid on the Instant Pot, making sure the steam-release valve is sealed. Press the Manual button, and set the Instant Pot for 5 minutes.

When the Instant Pot beeps, press Keep Warm/Cancel. Allow the Instant Pot to release its pressure naturally for 5 minutes. Using an oven mitt, open the steam-release valve. If there is any steam left over, allow it to release until the silver dial drops, then carefully open the lid.

Add the cheddar cheese, heavy cream and sour cream, stirring to combine.

Carefully pour the soup into a high-powered blender or leave it in the Instant Pot and use an immersion blender, leaving at least 3 inches (8 cm) of space from the top of the blender, then blend on low speed just until the soup is homogenous, about 10 seconds. You may need to do this in batches.

Taste the soup for seasoning and add more salt if you prefer it saltier. Transfer the soup to the Instant Pot and press Sauté. Bring the soup to a boil and stir it a few times. Press Keep Warm/Cancel. Stir in the crumbled bacon.

Serve the soup immediately as is or topped with additional shredded cheddar cheese and sliced jalapeños, if desired.

HOMEMADE CREAM OF MUSHROOM SOUP

PREP TIME: 20 MINUTES
COOK TIME: 13 MINUTES
TOTAL TIME: 33 MINUTES
YIELD: 4 TO 6 SERVINGS

This comforting soup has tons of caramelized, buttery mushrooms, vibrant herbs and a creamy broth base. No need to have this soup simmering on the stovetop for hours when it cooks so quickly in the Instant Pot!

3 tbsp (45 g) grass-fed butter

16 oz (454 g) mushrooms, cut into thirds, woody ends removed, divided

4 cloves garlic, finely chopped

1 large celery root cut into ¼-inch (6-mm) thick pieces

2 tbsp (10 g) finely chopped fresh Italian parsley, plus more if needed

1 tsp fresh thyme leaves

4 cups (960 ml) chicken or vegetable broth

1 tsp sea salt

½ tsp onion powder

1 cup (240 ml) heavy cream

Freshly ground black pepper (optional)

Add the butter to the Instant Pot and press Sauté. Once the butter has melted, add 8 ounces (227 g) of the mushrooms and sauté for 7 minutes, stirring occasionally, until the mushrooms begin to caramelize and turn golden brown. Add the garlic, stir and sauté for 1 minute. Press Keep Warm/Cancel.

Add the remaining 8 ounces (227 g) of mushrooms, celery root, parsley, thyme, broth, salt and onion powder to the Instant Pot. Stir to combine.

Place the lid on the Instant Pot, making sure the steam-release valve is sealed. Press the Manual button and set the Instant Pot for 5 minutes.

When the Instant Pot beeps, press Keep Warm/Cancel. Allow the Instant Pot to release its pressure naturally for 5 minutes. Using an oven mitt, open the steam-release valve. If there is any steam left over, allow it to release until the silver dial drops, then carefully open the lid.

Add the heavy cream, stirring to combine.

Carefully pour the soup into a high-powered blender or leave it in the Instant Pot and use an immersion blender, leaving at least 3 inches (8 cm) of space from the top of the blender, then pulse on low speed for 7 to 10 seconds, just until the mushrooms have been slightly chopped up but not fully pureed. You may need to do this in batches. Pour the soup back into the Instant Pot.

Taste the soup for seasoning and add more salt if you prefer it saltier. Press Sauté, bring the soup to a boil and stir it a few times. Press Keep Warm/Cancel.

Serve the soup immediately, as is or garnished with additional parsley and freshly ground black pepper, if desired.

THAI CARROT-COCONUT SOUP

PREP TIME: 20 MINUTES
COOK TIME: 18 MINUTES
TOTAL TIME: 38 MINUTES
YIELD: 4 TO 6 SERVINGS

This creamy pureed soup made with a kick of lemongrass and ginger captures the very essence of the bold flavors in Thai cuisine. It's the perfect soup to cozy up with and warm your chills.

3 tbsp (45 g) grass-fed butter or ghee or 3 tbsp (45 ml) avocado oil

½ small onion, finely chopped

4 cloves garlic, finely chopped

1 tbsp (9 g) finely chopped or grated fresh ginger

10 medium carrots, cut into thirds

4 cups (960 ml) chicken or vegetable broth

1 stalk lemongrass, cut in half lengthwise and quartered

1 tbsp (9 g) curry powder

1 tsp sea salt

½ tsp ground coriander

½ tsp dried thyme

⅛ tsp cayenne pepper

1 cup (240 ml) coconut milk

Finely chopped fresh cilantro (optional)

Lime wedges (optional)

Add the butter to the Instant Pot and press Sauté. Once the butter has melted, add the onion and sauté for 7 minutes, stirring occasionally, until the onion has begun to caramelize and turn golden brown. Add the garlic and ginger, stir and sauté for 1 minute. Press Keep Warm/Cancel.

Add the carrots, broth, lemongrass, curry powder, salt, coriander, thyme and cayenne to the Instant Pot. Stir to combine.

Place the lid on the Instant Pot, making sure the steam-release valve is sealed. Press the Manual button, and set the Instant Pot for 10 minutes.

When the Instant Pot beeps, press Keep Warm/Cancel. Allow the Instant Pot to release its pressure naturally for 5 minutes. Using an oven mitt, open the steam-release valve. If there is any steam left over, allow it to release until the silver dial drops, then carefully open the lid. With tongs or a spoon, remove and discard the lemongrass.

Carefully pour the soup into a high-powered blender or leave it in the Instant Pot and use an immersion blender, leaving at least 3 inches (8 cm) of space from the top of the blender, then blend on low speed just until the soup is homogenous, about 10 seconds. You may need to do this in batches.

Taste the soup for seasoning and add more salt if you prefer it saltier. Transfer the soup to the Instant Pot and press Sauté. Bring the soup to a boil and stir a few times. Press Keep Warm/Cancel. Add the coconut milk, stirring until fully incorporated.

Serve the soup immediately, as is or garnished with cilantro and lime wedges, if desired.

NOTE: Choose a curry powder that uses a blend of ingredients like coriander, turmeric, mustard, cumin, fenugreek, paprika, cayenne, cardamom, nutmeg, cinnamon and cloves (preferably an organic brand).

HEALTHY ZUCCHINI-MINT SOUP

PREP TIME: 20 MINUTES
COOK TIME: 8 MINUTES
TOTAL TIME: 28 MINUTES
YIELD: 4 TO 6 SERVINGS

Mint adds the most delicious flavor to this zucchini soup. It's meant to be enjoyed with extra sour cream, so don't skimp when you add that dollop to the top of the soup.

3 tbsp (45 g) grass-fed butter or ghee

5 cloves garlic, minced

½ tsp dried thyme

4 cups (496 g) diced zucchini

¾ cup (45 g) finely chopped fresh mint leaves

¼ cup (15 g) finely chopped Italian parsley

3 cups (720 ml) chicken or vegetable broth

1 tsp sea salt

1 cup (240 ml) heavy cream

1 cup (230 g) sour cream, plus more as needed

Extra virgin olive oil (optional)

Add the butter to the Instant Pot and press Sauté. Once the butter has melted, add the garlic and thyme and sauté for 1 minute, stirring occasionally. Add the zucchini, mint, parsley, chicken broth and salt, stirring to combine. Press Keep Warm/Cancel.

Place the lid on the Instant Pot, making sure the steam-release valve is sealed. Press the Manual button and set the Instant Pot for 7 minutes.

When the Instant Pot beeps, press Keep Warm/Cancel. Allow the Instant Pot to release its pressure naturally for 5 minutes. Using an oven mitt, open the steam-release valve. If there is any steam left over, allow it to release until the silver dial drops, then carefully open the lid.

Add the heavy cream and sour cream and stir until fully incorporated.

Carefully pour the soup into a high-powered blender or leave it in the Instant Pot and use an immersion blender, leaving at least 3 inches (8 cm) of space from the top of the blender, then blend on low speed just until the soup is homogeneous, about 5 seconds. You may need to do this in batches.

Taste the soup for seasoning and add more salt if you prefer it saltier. Transfer the soup to the Instant Pot and press Sauté. Bring the soup to a boil and stir it a few times. Press Keep Warm/Cancel.

Serve the soup immediately, topped with a dollop of additional sour cream and a drizzle of extra virgin olive oil, if desired.

COCONUT CURRY CAULIFLOWER SOUP

PREP TIME: 20 MINUTES
COOK TIME: 15 MINUTES
TOTAL TIME: 35 MINUTES
YIELD: 4 TO 6 SERVINGS

With hints of spicy ginger, flavorful curry and a little tang from zesty lime, this cauliflower soup provides a nice variety for the palate.

3 tbsp (45 g) grass-fed butter or ghee or 3 tbsp (45 ml) avocado oil

½ small onion, finely chopped

4 cloves garlic, finely chopped

1 tbsp (9 g) finely chopped or grated fresh ginger

4 cups (428 g) fresh or frozen cauliflower florets

5 cups (1.2 L) chicken or vegetable broth

2 tbsp (18 g) curry powder

1 tsp sea salt

½ tsp ground turmeric

½ tsp dried thyme

Juice of 1 small lime

1 cup (240 ml) coconut milk

½ cup (120 ml) heavy cream

Finely chopped fresh cilantro (optional)

Lime wedges (optional)

Add the butter to the Instant Pot and press Sauté. Once the butter has melted, add the onion and sauté for 7 minutes, stirring occasionally, until the onion has begun to caramelize and turn golden brown. Add the garlic and ginger, stir and sauté for 1 minute. Press Keep Warm/Cancel.

Add the cauliflower, chicken broth, curry powder, salt, turmeric, thyme and lime juice to the Instant Pot. Stir to combine.

Place the lid on the Instant Pot, making sure the steam-release valve is sealed. Press the Manual button and set the Instant Pot for 7 minutes.

When the Instant Pot beeps, press Keep Warm/Cancel. Allow the Instant Pot to release its pressure naturally for 5 minutes. Using an oven mitt, open the steam-release valve. If there is any steam left over, allow it to release until the silver dial drops, then carefully open the lid.

Carefully pour the soup into a high-powered blender or leave it in the Instant Pot and use an immersion blender, leaving at least 3 inches (8 cm) of space from the top of the blender, then blend on low speed just until the soup is homogenous, about 10 seconds. You may need to do this in batches.

Taste the soup for seasoning and add more salt if you prefer it saltier. Transfer the soup to the Instant Pot and press Sauté. Bring to a boil and stir it a few times. Then press Keep Warm/Cancel. Add the coconut milk and heavy cream, stirring until fully incorporated.

Serve the soup immediately as is or garnished with cilantro and lime wedges, if desired.

NOTES: Choose a curry powder that uses a blend of ingredients like coriander, turmeric, mustard, cumin, fenugreek, paprika, cayenne, cardamom, nutmeg, cinnamon and cloves (preferably an organic brand).

If you'd prefer this soup to be dairy-free, use ghee (which has had the dairy protein removed) or avocado oil and omit the heavy cream and use additional coconut milk instead.

CREAM OF BROCCOLI SOUP

PREP TIME: 15 MINUTES
COOK TIME: 5 MINUTES
TOTAL TIME: 20 MINUTES
YIELD: 4 TO 6 SERVINGS

This classic soup is known for being rich and simple. It's one of those soups elegant enough for dinner guests but comforting enough for a quiet evening alone. This version cooks so much quicker than stovetop cream of broccoli soup, coming together in fewer than thirty minutes.

3 tbsp (45 g) grass-fed butter

4 cups (624 g) fresh or frozen broccoli florets

4 cups (960 ml) chicken or vegetable broth

1 tsp sea salt

2 tsp (6 g) granulated garlic

½ tsp dried thyme

½ tsp dried dill

1 cup (240 ml) heavy cream

1 cup (230 g) sour cream, plus more as needed

Add the butter, broccoli, chicken broth, salt, granulated garlic, thyme and dill to the Instant Pot. Stir to combine.

Place the lid on the Instant Pot, making sure the steam-release valve is sealed. Press the Manual button, and set the Instant Pot for 5 minutes.

When the Instant Pot beeps, press Keep Warm/Cancel. Allow the Instant Pot to release its pressure naturally for 5 minutes. Using an oven mitt, open the steam-release valve. If there is any steam left over, allow it to release until the silver dial drops, then carefully open the lid.

Add the heavy cream and sour cream, stirring until they are incorporated.

Carefully pour three-quarters of the soup into a high-powered blender or leave it in the Instant Pot and use an immersion blender, reserving 1 cup (240 ml) of soup and leaving at least 3 inches (8 cm) of space from the top of the blender. Blend on low speed just until the soup is homogenous, about 5 seconds. Transfer the soup to the Instant Pot. Add the reserved soup and stir.

Taste the soup for seasoning and add more salt if you prefer it saltier. Serve the soup immediately as is or topped with a dollop of additional sour cream.

NOTE: If you prefer a completely smooth cream of broccoli soup, do not reserve the 1 cup (240 ml) of the soup—just blend it all.

FAT-PACKED CHEESY CAULIFLOWER BISQUE

PREP TIME: 15 MINUTES
COOK TIME: 5 MINUTES
TOTAL TIME: 20 MINUTES
YIELD: 4 TO 6 SERVINGS

This cauliflower bisque is complete bliss, packed with savory cheddar cheese and tangy sour cream. It cooks in just five minutes, and everything gets pureed to make a smooth, delectable bowl.

3 tbsp (45 g) grass-fed butter

4 cups (428 g) fresh or frozen cauliflower florets

3 cups (720 ml) chicken or vegetable broth

1 tsp sea salt

2 tsp (6 g) granulated garlic

½ tsp dried thyme

2½ cups (300 g) shredded cheddar cheese, plus more as needed

2 cups (480 ml) heavy cream

1 cup (230 g) sour cream

Add the butter, cauliflower, chicken broth, salt, granulated garlic and thyme to the Instant Pot. Stir to combine.

Place the lid on the Instant Pot, making sure the steam-release valve is sealed. Press the Manual button, and set the Instant Pot for 5 minutes.

When the Instant Pot beeps, press Keep Warm/Cancel. Allow the Instant Pot to release its pressure naturally for 5 minutes. Using an oven mitt, open the steam-release valve. If there is any steam left over, allow it to release until the silver dial drops, then carefully open the lid.

Add the cheddar cheese, heavy cream and sour cream, stirring until they are incorporated.

Carefully pour the soup into a high-powered blender or leave it in the Instant Pot and use an immersion blender, leaving at least 3 inches (8 cm) of space from the top of the blender, then blend on low speed just until the soup is homogenous, about 10 seconds. You may need to do this in batches.

Taste the soup for seasoning and add more salt if you prefer it saltier. Transfer the soup to the Instant Pot and press Sauté. Bring the soup to a boil and stir it a few times. Press Keep Warm/Cancel.

Serve immediately as is or topped with additional cheddar cheese.

SPICY CREAM CHEESE AND PUMPKIN SOUP WITH CRISPY BACON

PREP TIME: 20 MINUTES
COOK TIME: 18 MINUTES
TOTAL TIME: 38 MINUTES
YIELD: 4 TO 6 SERVINGS

This warming soup is perfect during the cold fall and winter months when pumpkins are in season. It's bursting with flavorful spices and heavenly little bites of bacon.

3 tbsp (45 g) grass-fed butter or ghee or 3 tbsp (45 ml) avocado oil

½ small onion, finely chopped

4 cloves garlic, finely chopped

1 tbsp (9 g) finely chopped or grated fresh ginger

Flesh of 2 small pie pumpkins, roasted or steamed (see Note)

4 cups (960 ml) chicken or vegetable broth

1 tbsp (9 g) curry powder

1 tsp sea salt

1 tsp dried thyme

1 tsp ground cumin

½ tsp ground cinnamon

¼ tsp cayenne pepper

½ cup (120 g) cream cheese

1 cup (240 ml) heavy cream

7 slices crispy cooked bacon, crumbled

Sour cream (optional)

Add the butter to the Instant Pot and press Sauté. Once the butter has melted, add the onion and sauté for 7 minutes, stirring occasionally, until the onion has begun to caramelize and turn golden brown. Add the garlic and ginger, stir and sauté for 1 minute. Press Keep Warm/Cancel.

Add the pumpkin flesh, chicken broth, curry powder, salt, thyme, cumin, cinnamon and cayenne to the Instant Pot. Stir to combine.

Place the lid on the Instant Pot, making sure the steam-release valve is sealed. Press the Manual button and set the Instant Pot for 10 minutes.

When the Instant Pot beeps, press Keep Warm/Cancel. Allow the Instant Pot to release its pressure naturally for 5 minutes. Using an oven mitt, open the steam-release valve. If there is any steam left over, allow it to release until the silver dial drops, then carefully open the lid.

Carefully pour the soup into a high-powered blender or leave it in the Instant Pot and use an immersion blender instead, leaving at least 3 inches (8 cm) of space from the top of the blender. Add the cream cheese. Blend on low speed just until the soup is homogenous, about 10 seconds. You may need to do this in batches.

Taste the soup for seasoning and add more salt if you prefer it saltier. Transfer the soup to the Instant Pot and press Sauté. Bring the soup to a boil and stir it a few times. Press Keep Warm/Cancel. Add the heavy cream and bacon, stirring until fully incorporated.

Serve the soup immediately, as is or topped with a dollop of sour cream, if desired.

NOTE: Two small pie pumpkins yield about 2½ cups (290 g) of pumpkin flesh. If you don't have time to roast the pumpkins (which takes about 40 minutes to 1 hour), try steaming them in the Instant Pot instead. Place the trivet in the Instant Pot, add 1 cup (240 ml) water and place a whole pie pumpkin (that fits in the Instant Pot) on top of the trivet. Place the lid on the Instant Pot with the steam valve closed and set it on Manual for 10 minutes. Allow the Instant Pot to release its pressure naturally for 10 minutes. This perfectly cooks the pumpkin and the skin peels off easily.

HERBED TURNIP-ARTICHOKE SOUP

PREP TIME: 20 MINUTES
COOK TIME: 5 MINUTES
TOTAL TIME: 25 MINUTES
YIELD: 4 TO 6 SERVINGS

This pureed soup is packed with sweet, peppery turnips, mild-flavored artichokes and lots of fresh herbs. It cooks in just five minutes in the Instant Pot.

3 tbsp (45 g) grass-fed butter

4 cups (520 g) peeled and cubed turnips

8 oz (224 g) artichoke hearts in water, drained

3 large celery ribs with leaves, cut into ¼-inch (6-mm) thick pieces

3 cups (720 ml) chicken or vegetable broth

1 tsp sea salt

1 tsp granulated garlic

¼ cup (15 g) finely chopped fresh Italian parsley, plus more as needed

2 tsp (2 g) fresh thyme leaves, plus more as needed

2 tsp (2 g) finely chopped fresh dill, plus more as needed

¼ cup (25 g) shredded Parmesan cheese

1½ cups (360 ml) heavy cream

1 cup (230 g) sour cream, plus more as needed

1 tbsp (3 g) finely chopped fresh chives, for garnish

Add the butter, turnips, artichoke hearts, celery, chicken broth, salt, granulated garlic, parsley, thyme and dill to the Instant Pot. Stir to combine.

Place the lid on the Instant Pot, making sure the steam-release valve is sealed. Press the Manual button, and set the Instant Pot for 5 minutes.

When the Instant Pot beeps, press Keep Warm/Cancel. Allow the Instant Pot to release its pressure naturally for 5 minutes. Using an oven mitt, open the steam-release valve. If there is any steam left over, allow it to release until the silver dial drops, then carefully open the lid.

Add the Parmesan cheese, heavy cream and sour cream, stirring until they are incorporated.

Carefully pour the soup into a high-powered blender or leave it in the Instant Pot and use an immersion blender, leaving at least 3 inches (8 cm) of space from the top of the blender, then blend on low speed just until the soup is homogenous, about 10 seconds. You may need to do this in batches.

Taste the soup for seasoning and add more salt if you prefer it saltier. Transfer the soup to the Instant Pot and press Sauté. Bring the soup to a boil and stir it a few times. Press Keep Warm/Cancel.

Serve the soup immediately as is or garnished with chives, additional parsley, thyme and dill or a dollop of additional sour cream.

CREAMY RADISH BISQUE

PREP TIME: 20 MINUTES
COOK TIME: 13 MINUTES
TOTAL TIME: 33 MINUTES
YIELD: 4 TO 6 SERVINGS

Raw radishes have a lovely peppery bite, but when they're cooked, they become sweet perfection. This delicate, savory bisque has hints of orange with vibrant herbs mixed in a creamy base.

3 tbsp (45 g) grass-fed butter

½ small onion, thinly sliced

3 cloves garlic, finely chopped

3 cups (348 g) halved radishes

1 cup (107 g) fresh or frozen cauliflower florets

3 cups (720 ml) chicken or vegetable broth

1 tsp sea salt

½ tsp freshly ground black pepper

3 tbsp (15 g) finely chopped fresh Italian parsley

Zest of 1 orange

1½ cups (360 ml) heavy cream

1 cup (230 g) sour cream, plus more as needed

2 tbsp (10 g) finely chopped fresh mint (optional)

1 tbsp (5 g) finely chopped fresh chives (optional)

1 to 3 radishes, thinly sliced (optional)

Add the butter to the Instant Pot and press Sauté. Once the butter has melted, add the onion and sauté for 7 minutes, stirring occasionally, until the onion has begun to caramelize and turn golden brown. Add the garlic, stir and sauté for 1 minute. Press Keep Warm/Cancel.

Add the radishes, cauliflower, chicken broth, salt, pepper, parsley and orange zest to the Instant Pot. Stir to combine.

Place the lid on the Instant Pot, making sure the steam-release valve is sealed. Press the Manual button, and set the Instant Pot for 5 minutes.

When the Instant Pot beeps, press Keep Warm/Cancel. Allow the Instant Pot to release its pressure naturally for 5 minutes. Using an oven mitt, open the steam-release valve. If there is any steam left over, allow it to release until the silver dial drops, then carefully open the lid.

Add the heavy cream and sour cream, stirring until they are incorporated.

Carefully pour the soup into a high-powered blender or leave it in the Instant Pot and use an immersion blender, leaving at least 3 inches (8 cm) of space from the top of the blender, then blend on low speed just until the soup is homogenous, about 10 seconds. You may need to do this in batches.

Taste the soup for seasoning and add more salt if you prefer it saltier. Transfer the soup to the Instant Pot and press Sauté. Bring the soup to a boil and stir it a few times. Press Keep Warm/Cancel.

Serve the soup immediately as is or topped with the mint, chives, radishes and a dollop of additional sour cream, if desired.

LOW-CARB CABBAGE SOUP

PREP TIME: 25 MINUTES
COOK TIME: 12 MINUTES
TOTAL TIME: 37 MINUTES
YIELD: 4 TO 6 SERVINGS

This vegetable soup is so simple and easy to make. It's jam-packed with slices of cabbage, zucchini and carrots and a bunch of herbs, which gives this broth-based soup lots of flavor. The prep is quick, and the soup cooks even quicker—before you know it, you'll be enjoying a bowl of this deliciousness topped with freshly grated nutty Parmesan.

3 tbsp (45 g) grass-fed butter or ghee or (45 ml) avocado oil

¼ cup (22 g) thinly sliced leeks (lower white parts only)

5 cloves garlic, finely chopped

1 small head green or savoy cabbage, thickly sliced

2 small zucchini, thickly sliced

1 large carrot, peeled and thickly sliced

1 tsp sea salt

Zest of 1 lemon

¼ cup (15 g) finely chopped fresh Italian parsley

¼ cup (15 g) finely chopped fresh cilantro

1 tbsp (5 g) finely chopped fresh dill

2 tsp (2 g) fresh thyme leaves

1 fresh or dried bay leaf

4 cups (960 ml) chicken or vegetable broth

Extra virgin olive oil, as needed

½ cup (50 g) shredded Parmesan cheese

Add the butter to the Instant Pot and press Sauté. Once the butter has melted, add the leeks and sauté for 7 minutes, stirring occasionally. Add the garlic and sauté for 1 minute, stirring occasionally. Press Keep Warm/Cancel.

Add the cabbage, zucchini, carrot, salt, lemon zest, parsley, cilantro, dill, thyme, bay leaf and chicken broth to the Instant Pot. Stir to combine.

Place the lid on the Instant Pot, making sure the steam-release valve is sealed. Press the Manual button, and set the Instant Pot for 4 minutes.

When the Instant Pot beeps, press Keep Warm/Cancel. Using an oven mitt, "quick release" the steam-release valve. When the steam stops venting and the silver dial drops, carefully open the lid.

Taste the soup for seasoning and add more salt if you prefer it saltier. Remove and discard the bay leaf.

Drizzle each serving with the extra virgin olive oil and garnish with the Parmesan cheese. Serve immediately.

CREAM OF CELERY SOUP

PREP TIME: 20 MINUTES
COOK TIME: 21 MINUTES
TOTAL TIME: 41 MINUTES
YIELD: 4 TO 6 SERVINGS

Relive the nostalgia of your favorite childhood soup with real-food ingredients—no can opener required! The refreshing burst of celery with herbs and a hint of white wine makes for a simple feast.

3 tbsp (45 g) grass-fed butter

½ small onion, finely chopped

3 cloves garlic, finely chopped

½ cup (120 ml) dry white wine

7 large celery ribs, finely chopped

1 cup (156 g) peeled and cubed celery root

1 tbsp (5 g) finely chopped fresh Italian parsley, plus more as needed

1 tsp fresh thyme leaves, plus more as needed

1 tsp fresh dill, finely chopped, plus more as needed

4 cups (960 ml) chicken or vegetable broth

1 tsp sea salt

1½ cups (360 ml) heavy cream

Sour cream (optional)

Add the butter to the Instant Pot and press Sauté. Once the butter has melted, add the onion and sauté for 7 minutes, stirring occasionally, until the onion has begun to caramelize and turn golden brown. Add the garlic, stir and sauté for 1 minute. Add the white wine and stir. Press Keep Warm/Cancel.

Add the celery, celery root, parsley, thyme, dill, chicken broth and salt to the Instant Pot. Stir to combine.

Place the lid on the Instant Pot, making sure the steam-release valve is sealed. Press the Manual button, and set the Instant Pot for 13 minutes.

When the Instant Pot beeps, press Keep Warm/Cancel. Allow the Instant Pot to release its pressure naturally for 5 minutes. Using an oven mitt, open the steam-release valve. If there is any steam left over, allow it to release until the silver dial drops, then carefully open the lid.

Carefully pour the soup into a high-powered blender or leave it in the Instant Pot and use an immersion blender, leaving at least 3 inches (8 cm) of space from the top of the blender, then blend on low speed just until the soup is homogenous, about 10 seconds. You may need to do this in batches.

Taste the soup for seasoning and add more salt if you prefer it saltier. Transfer the soup to the Instant Pot. Press Sauté. Bring the soup to a boil and stir it a few times. Press Keep Warm/Cancel. Add the heavy cream, stirring until it is incorporated.

Serve the soup immediately, as is or garnished with additional parsley, thyme and dill or a dollop of sour cream, if desired.

NOURISHING CRAB BISQUE

PREP TIME: 20 MINUTES
COOK TIME: 16 MINUTES
TOTAL TIME: 36 MINUTES
YIELD: 4 TO 6 SERVINGS

Fresh crab always reminds us of Bodega Bay, California, a place we both visited as kids and where we eventually got married. We love bringing the flavors of the sea home and creating meals with it, like this pureed crab bisque.

3 tbsp (45 g) grass-fed butter

½ small onion, diced

3 cloves garlic, finely chopped

½ cup (120 ml) dry white wine

2 cups (214 g) fresh or frozen cauliflower florets

1 large celery rib, cut into ¼-inch (6-mm) thick pieces

1 tsp sea salt

½ tsp dried thyme

⅛ tsp freshly ground black pepper

2 dried bay leaves

Zest of 1 lemon

¼ cup (15 g) finely chopped fresh Italian parsley

3 cups (720 ml) fish or crab stock or chicken or vegetable broth

1 lb (454 g) cooked crabmeat, plus more as needed

1½ cups (360 ml) heavy cream

2 tbsp (10 g) finely chopped chives, plus more as needed

Sour cream (optional)

Add the butter to the Instant Pot and press Sauté. Once the butter has melted, add the onion and sauté for 5 minutes, stirring occasionally. Add the garlic and sauté for 1 minute, stirring occasionally. Add the white wine and stir. Press the Keep Warm/Cancel button.

Add the cauliflower, celery, salt, thyme, pepper, bay leaves, lemon zest, parsley, fish stock and crabmeat to the Instant Pot. Stir to combine.

Place the lid on the Instant Pot, making sure the steam-release valve is sealed. Press the Manual button and set the Instant Pot for 10 minutes.

When the Instant Pot beeps, press Keep Warm/Cancel. Allow the Instant Pot to release its pressure naturally for 5 minutes. Using an oven mitt, open the steam-release valve. If there is any steam left over, allow it to release until the silver dial drops, then carefully open the lid. With tongs or a spoon, remove and discard the bay leaves.

Carefully pour the soup into a high-powered blender or leave it in the Instant Pot and use an immersion blender, leaving at least 3 inches (8 cm) of space from the top of the blender, then blend on low speed just until the soup is homogenous, about 10 seconds. You may need to do this in batches.

Taste the soup for seasoning and add more salt if you prefer it saltier. Transfer the soup to the Instant Pot and press Sauté. Bring the soup to a boil and stir it a few times. Press Keep Warm/Cancel. Add the heavy cream and chives, stirring to combine.

If desired, garnish the soup with additional crabmeat, chives or a dollop of sour cream. Serve immediately.

MAGGIE B'S LOW-CARB SEAFOOD STEW

PREP TIME: 25 MINUTES
COOK TIME: 14 MINUTES
TOTAL TIME: 39 MINUTES
YIELD: 4 TO 6 SERVINGS

My mom read the children's book *The Maggie B* to me when I was a little girl, and now I read it to my kids. Our favorite part is when the little girl makes a beautiful sea stew with homegrown produce and a lobster and sea bass that she caught. She serves the soup to her little brother with freshly baked muffins that they dip in the stew. This is our version of the sea stew from this sweet story.

3 tbsp (45 g) grass-fed butter or ghee or (45 ml) avocado oil

½ small onion, diced

5 cloves garlic, finely chopped

½ small head green or savoy cabbage, thickly sliced

3 medium tomatoes, seeds removed, coarsely chopped

2 medium carrots, peeled and thickly sliced

1 tsp sea salt

2 fresh or dried bay leaves

Zest of 1 lemon

¼ cup (15 g) finely chopped fresh Italian parsley, plus more as needed

1 tbsp (5 g) finely chopped fresh dill, plus more as needed

2 tsp (2 g) fresh thyme leaves, plus more as needed

1 tsp finely chopped fresh rosemary, plus more as needed

4 cups (960 ml) fish or lobster stock

1½ lb (680 g) sea bass, cut into 3-inch (8-cm) pieces

1 (5 to 6-oz [140 to 168-g]) frozen lobster tail

Extra virgin olive oil

Add the butter to the Instant Pot and press Sauté. Once the butter has melted, add the onion and sauté for 7 minutes, stirring occasionally, until the onion is caramelized. Add the garlic and sauté for 1 minute, stirring occasionally. Press Keep Warm/Cancel.

Add the cabbage, tomatoes, carrots, salt, bay leaves, lemon zest, parsley, dill, thyme, rosemary, fish stock, sea bass and lobster to the Instant Pot. Stir to combine.

Place the lid on the Instant Pot, making sure the steam-release valve is sealed. Press the Manual button, and set the Instant Pot for 6 minutes.

When the Instant Pot beeps, press Keep Warm/Cancel. Using an oven mitt, "quick release" the steam-release valve. When the steam stops venting and the silver dial drops, carefully open the lid.

Taste the stew for seasoning and add more salt if you prefer it saltier. Remove and discard the bay leaves.

Garnish the stew with additional parsley, dill, thyme and rosemary and drizzle it with the extra virgin olive oil. Serve immediately.

NOTES: Chicken or vegetable broth can be substituted for the fish stock if needed.

If sea bass isn't available locally, you can substitute it with halibut or another whitefish.

Use the Monterey Bay Aquarium's Seafood Watch website or app to make sure you choose low-mercury, sustainable fish.

CREAMY CHICKEN, ROSEMARY AND MUSHROOM SOUP

PREP TIME: 25 MINUTES
COOK TIME: 22 MINUTES
TOTAL TIME: 47 MINUTES
YIELD: 6 SERVINGS

With tender bites of chicken mixed into a rustic pureed cream base full of mushrooms, celery, rosemary and hints of lemon and white wine, this soup will have you going back for a second bowl.

3 tbsp (45 g) grass-fed butter or ghee

½ small onion, diced

1½ lb (680 g) mushrooms, cut into thirds, woody ends removed

5 cloves garlic, finely chopped

1 cup (240 ml) dry white wine

3 large celery ribs with leaves, cut into ¼-inch (6-mm) thick pieces

1 tsp sea salt

Zest of 1 lemon

¼ cup (15 g) finely chopped fresh Italian parsley, plus more as needed

2 tbsp (10 g) finely chopped fresh rosemary, plus more as needed

2 tsp (2 g) fresh thyme leaves, plus more as needed

2 (4-oz [112-g]) boneless and skinless chicken breasts

4 cups (960 ml) chicken or vegetable broth

1½ cups (360 ml) heavy cream

Extra virgin olive oil

Add the butter to the Instant Pot and press Sauté. Once the butter has melted, add the onion and mushrooms and sauté for 9 minutes, stirring occasionally, until the vegetables are caramelized. Add the garlic and sauté for 1 minute, stirring occasionally. Add the wine to deglaze the pot, scraping up any browned bits with a wooden spoon. Press the Keep Warm/Cancel button.

Add the celery, salt, lemon zest, parsley, rosemary, thyme, chicken breasts and chicken broth to the Instant Pot, making sure the chicken is submerged in the liquid.

Place the lid on the Instant Pot, making sure the steam-release valve is sealed. Press the Manual button, and set the Instant Pot for 12 minutes.

When the Instant Pot beeps, press Keep Warm/Cancel. Using an oven mitt, "quick release" the steam-release valve. When the steam stops venting and the silver dial drops, carefully open the lid.

With tongs, remove the chicken breasts from the Instant Pot and place them on a plate or cutting board. Chop the chicken into bite-size chunks, then set aside.

Carefully pour three-quarters of the soup into a high-powered blender or leave it in the Instant Pot and use an immersion blender, leaving at least 3 inches (8 cm) of space from the top of the blender. Blend on low speed just until the soup is roughly pureed, about 5 seconds—the mushrooms should still be slightly chunky. You may need to do this in batches.

Taste the soup for seasoning and add more salt if you prefer it saltier. Transfer the soup and chicken to the Instant Pot. Add the heavy cream and press Sauté. Bring the soup to a boil and stir it a few times. Press Keep Warm/Cancel.

Garnish the soup with additional parsley, rosemary and thyme and drizzle it with the extra virgin olive oil. Serve immediately.

CLASSIC BEEF AND VEGGIE STEW

PREP TIME: 25 MINUTES
COOK TIME: 50 MINUTES
TOTAL TIME: 75 MINUTES
YIELD: 6 SERVINGS

Rich and hearty, overflowing with tender chunks of meat, bites of veggies and lots of herbs in a red wine–broth base, this stew is sure to please. The best part of this version is that it doesn't need to simmer for hours on the stove—it cooks so much faster with the help of the Instant Pot.

4 tbsp (60 g) grass-fed butter or ghee or (60 ml) avocado oil, divided

2 lb (908 g) grass-fed beef stew meat, cut into 1-inch (2.5-cm) chunks

½ small onion, diced

8 oz (224 g) mushrooms, halved or cut into thirds, woody ends removed

5 cloves garlic, finely chopped

1 cup (240 ml) dry red wine

4 medium tomatoes, seeds removed, coarsely chopped

3 large celery ribs with leaves, cut into ¼-inch (6-mm) pieces

2 medium carrots, peeled and thickly sliced

1 tsp sea salt

½ tsp freshly ground black pepper

2 fresh or dried bay leaves

¼ cup (15 g) finely chopped fresh Italian parsley

2 tsp (2 g) fresh thyme leaves

2 tsp (2 g) finely chopped fresh rosemary

2½ cups (600 ml) beef or chicken broth

Add 2 tablespoons (30 g) of the butter to the Instant Pot and press Sauté. Once the butter has melted, add the stew meat and brown the meat about 5 minutes, stirring occasionally. You might have to do this in batches. Using tongs or a spoon, remove the browned stew meat, transfer it to a plate and set aside. Add the remaining 2 tablespoons (30 g) butter, then add the onion and mushrooms and sauté for 9 minutes, stirring occasionally. Add the garlic and sauté for 1 minute, stirring occasionally. Add the red wine to deglaze the pot, scraping up any browned bits with a wooden spoon. Press Keep Warm/Cancel.

Add the tomatoes, celery, carrots, salt, pepper, bay leaves, parsley, thyme, rosemary, beef broth and the browned meat to the Instant Pot. Stir to combine.

Place the lid on the Instant Pot, making sure the steam-release valve is sealed. Press the Manual button, and set the Instant Pot for 35 minutes.

When the Instant Pot beeps, press Keep Warm/Cancel. Using an oven mitt, "quick release" the steam-release valve. When the steam stops venting and the silver dial drops, carefully open the lid.

Taste the stew for seasoning and add more salt if you prefer it saltier. Remove and discard the bay leaves.

Serve the stew immediately.

ITALIAN WEDDING SOUP

PREP TIME: 30 MINUTES
COOK TIME: 21 MINUTES
TOTAL TIME: 51 MINUTES
YIELD: 6 SERVINGS

Wedding soup is a "marriage" between green veggies and meatballs. It's common to see this soup with breadcrumbs or rice in the meatballs and small pasta in the soup, but you won't find any in this delicious grain-free version.

MEATBALLS

1 lb (454 g) grass-fed ground beef or chicken

¼ cup (15 g) finely chopped fresh Italian parsley

2 tbsp (10 g) finely chopped fresh mint

1 tsp sea salt

1 large egg

¾ cup (75 g) shredded Parmesan cheese

SOUP

4 tbsp (60 g) grass-fed butter or ghee or (60 ml) avocado oil

½ small onion, diced

1 small bulb fennel, thinly sliced

5 cloves garlic, finely chopped

2 medium tomatoes, seeds removed, coarsely chopped

4 large celery ribs with leaves, cut into ¼-inch (6-mm) thick pieces

2 small zucchini, thickly sliced

1 tsp sea salt

Zest of 1 lemon

¼ cup (15 g) finely chopped fresh Italian parsley

2 tbsp (10 g) finely chopped fresh mint

1 tsp fresh thyme leaves

4 cups (960 ml) chicken or vegetable broth

4 cups (120 g) fresh spinach

Shredded or grated Parmesan cheese, as needed

To make the meatballs, in a large bowl, combine the ground beef, parsley, mint, salt, egg and Parmesan cheese and gently mix until everything is incorporated. Roll the mixture into 2-inch (5-cm) meatballs. Set them aside on a plate.

To make the soup, add the butter to the Instant Pot and press Sauté. Once the butter has melted, add the onion and fennel and sauté for 7 minutes, until the vegetables are caramelized, stirring occasionally. Add the garlic and sauté for 1 minute, stirring occasionally. Press Keep Warm/Cancel.

Add the tomatoes, celery, zucchini, salt, lemon zest, parsley, mint, thyme and chicken broth to the Instant Pot. Stir to combine. Gently add the meatballs, making sure they're submerged in the liquid.

Place the lid on the Instant Pot, making sure the steam-release valve is sealed. Press the Manual button, and set the Instant Pot for 13 minutes.

When the Instant Pot beeps, press Keep Warm/Cancel. Allow the Instant Pot to release its pressure naturally for 5 minutes. Using an oven mitt, open the steam-release valve. If there is any steam left over, allow it to release until the silver dial drops, then carefully open the lid.

Add the spinach and stir until all of the spinach has wilted. Taste the soup for seasoning and add more salt if you prefer it saltier.

Serve the soup immediately, garnished with the Parmesan cheese.

PROTEIN-PACKED CIOPPINO

PREP TIME: 25 MINUTES
COOK TIME: 12 MINUTES
TOTAL TIME: 37 MINUTES
YIELD: 4 TO 6 SERVINGS

This hearty fish stew originated in San Francisco, a city that I visited often as a little girl, especially during the holidays. I later spent part of my childhood there. The city is known for being rich in culture and offering a wide variety of different cuisines, but one dish that it's especially famous for is cioppino, a brothy seafood stew originally developed by Italian immigrants in the North Beach district.

2 tbsp (30 g) grass-fed butter or ghee or (30 ml) avocado oil

½ small onion, diced

1 small bulb fennel, thinly sliced

5 cloves garlic, finely chopped

1½ cups (360 ml) dry white wine

4 medium tomatoes, seeds removed, coarsely chopped

3 large celery ribs with leaves, cut into ¼-inch (6-mm) thick pieces

1 tsp sea salt

Zest of 1 lemon

¼ cup (15 g) finely chopped fresh Italian parsley, plus more as needed

1 tbsp (5 g) finely chopped fresh basil, plus more as needed

2 tsp (2 g) fresh thyme leaves, plus more as needed

2 lb (908 g) assorted fresh seafood like clams, cleaned; mussels, cleaned; jumbo shrimp, peeled and deveined and scallops

1 lb (454 g) Dungeness crab or canned lump crabmeat

4 cups (960 ml) fish or crab stock

Extra virgin olive oil, as needed

Add the butter to the Instant Pot and press Sauté. Once the butter has melted, add the onion and fennel and sauté for 7 minutes, until the vegetables are caramelized, stirring occasionally. Add the garlic and sauté for 1 minute, stirring occasionally. Add the wine to deglaze the pot, scraping up any browned bits with a wooden spoon. Press Keep Warm/Cancel.

Add the tomatoes, celery, salt, lemon zest, parsley, basil, thyme, assorted seafood, Dungeness crab and fish stock to the Instant Pot. Stir to combine.

Place the lid on the Instant Pot, making sure the steam-release valve is sealed. Press the Manual button, and set the Instant Pot for 4 minutes.

When the Instant Pot beeps, press Keep Warm/Cancel. Using an oven mitt, "quick release" the steam-release valve. When the steam stops venting and the silver dial drops, carefully open the lid.

Taste the cioppino for seasoning and add more salt if you prefer it saltier. With tongs or a spoon, remove and discard any clams or mussels that did not open.

Garnish the cioppino with additional parsley, basil and thyme and drizzle it with extra virgin olive oil. Serve immediately.

NOTES: Use the Monterey Bay Aquarium's Seafood Watch website or app to make sure you choose low-mercury, sustainable seafood.

This stew is meant to be served with something to dip in and absorb the broth, so enjoy it with low-carb biscuits or low-carb bread.

HEALTHY FIXINGS TO COMPLEMENT THE MEAL

A meal isn't complete without a complementary side dish to round it off. Whereas most side dishes are recognized as the trusty "sidekick" to the main course, the delicious co-captains in this chapter are hearty enough to be a meal in themselves.

Pair the Low-Carb Turnip and Celery Root Mash (page 133) with the Healthy Pesto Chicken Alfredo (page 14) or help yourself to a generous scoop of High-Fat Greek Spinach Dip (page 141) à la carte.

If you're looking for a healthy alternative to a tasty traditional classic, take a batch of the "Just Like Potato" Cauli Salad (page 137) to your next picnic, potluck or barbecue.

The best part about making side dishes in the Instant Pot is that they're all done in mere minutes. It's not uncommon to have the main dish cooking in one of our Instant Pots while we have a side dish cooking in another. Sometimes the side dish is done so fast that we enjoy it as an appetizer before the meal.

LOW-CARB TURNIP AND CELERY ROOT MASH

PREP TIME: **20 MINUTES**
COOK TIME: **6 MINUTES**
TOTAL TIME: **26 MINUTES**
YIELD: **6 TO 8 SERVINGS**

Sometimes we just need that classic comforting side of mashed potatoes. This lower-carb turnip and celery root mash is a wonderful alternative. It's so flavorful, and it's extra tasty topped with a pat of butter or drizzled with homemade gravy.

1 cup (240 ml) filtered water

5 medium turnips, peeled and cut into large cubes

5 small celery roots, peeled and cut into large cubes

4 tbsp (60 g) grass-fed butter or ghee

2 tbsp (30 ml) bone broth, chicken stock or vegetable broth

2 sprigs fresh thyme, stems removed

¾ tsp sea salt

½ tsp granulated garlic or garlic powder

Add the water to the Instant Pot. Place a steamer insert basket inside the pot and layer the turnips and celery roots on top of the steamer insert.

Place the lid on the Instant Pot, making sure the steam-release valve is sealed. Press the Manual button, and set the Instant Pot for 5 minutes.

When the Instant Pot beeps, press Keep Warm/Cancel. Allow the Instant Pot to release its pressure naturally for 10 minutes. Using an oven mitt, open the steam-release valve. If there is any steam left over, allow it to release until the silver dial drops, then carefully open the lid.

Using a large slotted spoon, carefully remove the vegetables and place them into a blender or food processor. Add the butter, bone broth, thyme, salt and granulated garlic. Pulse or blend from 30 seconds to 1 minute or until the mixture is completely smooth.

Serve the mash immediately.

HEALTHY BABA GHANOUSH

PREP TIME: **20 MINUTES**
COOK TIME: **11 MINUTES**
TOTAL TIME: **31 MINUTES**
YIELD: **4 SERVINGS**

I have had a fondness for baba ghanoush since my teen years. An old childhood friend introduced me to it at a local Lebanese restaurant we used to go to, and ever since it's been a favorite. If you've never had it before, it's similar to and has the same texture as hummus, but it's made with a base of roasted eggplant. It's absolutely heavenly and cooks so quickly with the help of the Instant Pot.

2 large purple eggplants

4 cloves garlic, peeled

¼ cup (60 ml) filtered water

3 tbsp (45 g) roasted tahini

Zest of 1 lemon

3 tbsp (45 ml) fresh lemon juice

¼ cup (15 g) Italian parsley, finely chopped, plus more as needed

1 tsp sea salt

¼ cup (60 ml) extra virgin olive oil, plus more as needed

Preheat the oven to broil.

Place the eggplants and garlic on a large baking sheet and place the baking sheet under the broiler, allowing both eggplants to roast on each side until the skin becomes browned but not burned, for 1 to 2 minutes per side. Carefully remove the baking sheet from the oven. With tongs, transfer the hot eggplants to a cutting board and set the roasted garlic to the side. Cut the eggplant into thick slices widthwise.

Add the eggplants and water to the Instant Pot.

Place the lid on the Instant Pot, making sure the steam-release valve is sealed. Press the Manual button, and set the Instant Pot for 3 minutes.

When the Instant Pot beeps, press Keep Warm/Cancel. Using an oven mitt, "quick release" the steam-release valve. When the steam stops venting and the silver dial drops, carefully open the lid.

Transfer the eggplants to a food processor fitted with a steel blade. Add the roasted garlic, tahini, lemon zest, lemon juice, parsley and salt. Place the lid on the food processor and pulse a couple of times. With the food processor running, slowly add the oil 1 tablespoon (15 ml) at a time through the processor's feed tube until the baba ghanoush reaches the desired texture.

Serve the baba ghanoush immediately, garnished with additional parsley and oil.

NOTE: I use the common globe eggplant for this recipe, although any variety of eggplant can be used.

"JUST LIKE POTATO" CAULI SALAD

PREP TIME: **20 MINUTES**
COOK TIME: **2 MINUTES**
TOTAL TIME: **22 MINUTES**
YIELD: **6 TO 8 SERVINGS**

My family loves potato salad—my husband and I both grew up enjoying it. But potatoes don't love our bodies, so we had to come up with something similar to satisfy our cravings. This "potato" cauli salad is based on my Southern grandma's secret potato salad recipe, sans the mayo. You'll be savoring every bite!

1½ cups (345 g) sour cream

3 tbsp (45 g) sugar-free Dijon or horseradish mustard

1 tbsp (15 ml) apple cider vinegar

1 tsp sea salt

3 tbsp (15 g) fresh dill, finely chopped

1 tbsp (5 g) Italian parsley, finely chopped

1 cup (143 g) sugar-free fermented pickles, diced

5 large celery ribs, cut into ¼-inch (6-mm) thick pieces

½ small onion, diced (optional)

1 cup (240 ml) filtered water

2 large heads cauliflower, stalks and leaves removed, cut into florets

In a large bowl, combine the sour cream, mustard, vinegar, salt, dill, parsley, pickles, celery and onion, finishing with the onion on top. Set aside.

Add the water to the Instant Pot. Place a steamer insert inside the pot and layer the cauliflower florets on top of the steamer insert.

Place the lid on the Instant Pot, making sure the steam-release valve is sealed. Press the Manual button, and set the Instant Pot for 2 minutes.

When the Instant Pot beeps, press Keep Warm/Cancel. Using an oven mitt, "quick release" the steam-release valve. When the steam stops venting and the silver dial drops, carefully open the lid.

Carefully remove the steamer insert with the cauliflower. Transfer the steamed cauliflower to the bowl with the sour cream mixture. Allow the hot cauliflower to sit on top of the onion for 5 minutes (this gently cooks the onion). Gently fold together all the ingredients until everything has been evenly distributed. Cover the bowl and place it in the refrigerator until the salad is chilled, 2 to 4 hours.

NOTES: My family isn't a fan of hard-boiled eggs in "potato" salad, but if you are, by all means go ahead and add 2 to 4 chopped hard-boiled eggs to the salad.

The onion is completely optional. If you still like the flavor of the onion but would prefer for the salad to be lower-carb, use 1 to 2 diced scallions instead of the onion.

GARLIC-HERB BRUSSELS SPROUTS

PREP TIME: 15 MINUTES
COOK TIME: 7 MINUTES
TOTAL TIME: 22 MINUTES
YIELD: 8 TO 10 SERVINGS

Cook your Brussels sprouts to perfection in the Instant Pot! This fan-favorite veggie is made easy with the press of the button and is sure to please—get your Brussels sprouts while they're in season so you don't miss out.

1 cup (240 ml) filtered water

2 lb (908 g) Brussels sprouts, trimmed and halved

4 tbsp (60 g) grass-fed butter or ghee or (60 ml) avocado oil

5 cloves garlic, minced

1 tsp sea salt

3 tbsp (45 ml) fresh lemon juice

1 tbsp (5 g) minced chives

1 tbsp (3 g) fresh Italian parsley, finely chopped

1 tsp fresh thyme leaves

1 tsp fresh dill, finely chopped

Add the water to the Instant Pot. Place the steamer insert inside the pot and layer the Brussels sprouts on top of the steamer insert.

Place the lid on the Instant Pot, making sure the steam-release valve is sealed. Press the Manual button, and set the Instant Pot for 2 minutes.

When the Instant Pot beeps, press Keep Warm/Cancel. Allow the Instant Pot to release its pressure naturally for 10 minutes. Using an oven mitt, open the steam-release valve. If there is any steam left over, allow it to release until the silver dial drops, then carefully open the lid.

Carefully remove the Brussels sprouts and steamer insert, setting the Brussels sprouts aside. Pour out the water that remains in the pot and return to the Instant Pot. Add the butter to the Instant Pot and press Sauté. Once the butter has melted, add the garlic and sauté for 1 minute, stirring occasionally. Add the Brussels sprouts and salt, sautéing until the Brussels sprouts start to turn golden brown, about 3 minutes. Add the lemon juice and sauté for 1 minute. Press Keep Warm/Cancel and add the chives, parsley, thyme and dill, stirring to combine.

Serve the Brussels sprouts immediately.

NOTE: Fresh basil or rosemary can be substituted for any of the herbs.

HIGH-FAT GREEK SPINACH DIP

PREP TIME: 25 MINUTES
COOK TIME: 12 MINUTES
TOTAL TIME: 37 MINUTES
YIELD: 4 TO 6 SERVINGS

Who doesn't enjoy a satisfying hot dip from time to time? When I was growing up, all kinds of hot dips were staple appetizers at any holiday party or family gathering. My husband and I love them too; they're perfect for a date night at home. We especially love this creamy Greek spinach dip. It is packed with good-for-you spinach, herbs, a bit of zesty lemon and, of course, some feta.

Butter, as needed

10 oz (280 g) frozen chopped spinach, thawed and moisture squeezed out

4 oz (113 g) cream cheese, softened

1 cup (230 g) sour cream

½ cup (75 g) crumbled feta cheese, divided

½ cup (56 g) shredded mozzarella cheese

½ cup (50 g) shredded Parmesan cheese

Zest of 1 lemon

2 tbsp (30 ml) fresh lemon juice

1 tsp sea salt

1 tsp granulated garlic or powder

3 scallions (white and light green parts only), finely chopped

½ cup (30 g) finely chopped fresh Italian parsley

2 tsp (2 g) dried dill

¼ tsp dried thyme

1 cup (240 ml) filtered water

Use butter to grease a 1½-quart (1.5-L) baking dish with a glass lid that fits in the Instant Pot. Set aside.

In a large bowl, combine the spinach, cream cheese, sour cream, ¼ cup (38 g) of the feta cheese, mozzarella cheese, Parmesan cheese, lemon zest, lemon juice, salt, granulated garlic, scallions, parsley, dill and thyme. Stir to combine.

Add the spinach mixture to the prepared baking dish. Evenly sprinkle the remaining ¼ cup (38 g) of the feta cheese on top of the spinach dip. Place the lid on top of the baking dish.

Place the Instant Pot trivet inside the Instant Pot. Pour the water into the Instant Pot. Carefully transfer the covered baking dish to the Instant Pot on top of the trivet.

Place the lid on the Instant Pot, making sure the steam-release valve is sealed. Press the Manual button, and set the Instant Pot for 10 minutes.

When the Instant Pot beeps, press Keep Warm/Cancel. Using an oven mitt, "quick release" the steam-release valve. When the steam stops venting and the silver dial drops, carefully open the lid.

Carefully remove the baking dish from the Instant Pot and remove the lid.

Serve the dip immediately.

Alternatively, if you prefer a browned dip, place the baking dish on a medium baking sheet and place it under a preheated broiler for 1 to 2 minutes, just until the top becomes bubbly and golden brown. Serve the dip immediately.

NOTE: If you don't have a lid for your baking dish, you can place a piece of parchment paper over the top, then cover it securely with foil.

CHEESE LOVERS' STUFFED POBLANO PEPPERS

PREP TIME: **25 MINUTES**
COOK TIME: **5 MINUTES**
TOTAL TIME: **30 MINUTES**
YIELD: **4 SERVINGS**

Jam-packed with cheesy goodness, these stuffed poblano peppers are sure to please. The seeds are removed from these milder peppers, so even those of you who prefer less heat can enjoy this dish.

8 medium poblano peppers

8 oz (224 g) cream cheese, softened

1½ cups (167 g) shredded mozzarella cheese

½ tsp sea salt

¼ tsp dried thyme

1 cup (240 ml) filtered water

Cut a slit down the length of one side of the peppers, taking care not to slice through the whole pepper. Using a paring knife or small spoon, scrape out the peppers' seeds and discard them. Set the cleaned peppers aside.

In a medium bowl, combine the cream cheese, mozzarella cheese, salt and thyme. Stir to combine.

Use a small spoon to stuff the cheese mixture into the peppers. Arrange the stuffed peppers in stacked layers in a 1½-quart (1.5-L) baking dish with a glass lid that fits in the Instant Pot. Place the lid on top of the baking dish.

Place the Instant Pot trivet inside the Instant Pot. Pour the water into the Instant Pot.

Carefully transfer the covered baking dish to the Instant Pot on top of the trivet.

Place the lid on the Instant Pot, making sure the steam-release valve is sealed. Press the Manual button, and set the Instant Pot for 5 minutes.

When the Instant Pot beeps, press Keep Warm/Cancel. Using an oven mitt, "quick release" the steam-release valve. When the steam stops venting and the silver dial drops, carefully open the lid.

Carefully remove the baking dish from the Instant Pot and remove the lid.

Using a large serving spoon, carefully transfer the peppers to a serving dish. Serve the peppers immediately.

Alternatively, if you prefer, place the peppers on a medium baking sheet and place it under a preheated broiler for 1 to 2 minutes, just until the tops become golden brown. Serve the peppers immediately.

NOTE: If you don't have a lid for your baking dish, you can place a piece of parchment paper over the top, then cover it securely with foil.

GARLIC-GINGER BOK CHOY

PREP TIME: **15 MINUTES**
COOK TIME: **6 MINUTES**
TOTAL TIME: **21 MINUTES**
YIELD: **4 SERVINGS**

Spinach and kale seem to be the "supergreens" that everyone goes crazy for, but we think bok choy should be given a chance. It's truly one of the most delicious vegetables and a versatile side dish for many meals. This simple version is a favorite in our home and as an added bonus, it cooks quickly in the Instant Pot.

3 tbsp (45 g) grass-fed butter or ghee

4 cloves garlic, minced

1 (½-inch [13-mm]) piece fresh ginger, peeled and minced

¾ tsp sea salt

1 tbsp (15 ml) coconut aminos or liquid aminos

½ cup (120 ml) chicken or vegetable broth

7 baby bok choy, cut in half down the middle

Add the butter to the Instant Pot and press Sauté. Once the butter has melted, add the garlic and sauté for 1 minute, stirring occasionally. Add the ginger and sauté for about 3 minutes, until fragrant. Press Keep Warm/Cancel.

Add the sea salt, aminos and broth to the Instant Pot, then add the bok choy.

Place the lid on the Instant Pot, making sure the steam-release valve is sealed. Press the Manual button and set the Instant Pot for 3 minutes.

When the Instant Pot beeps, press Keep Warm/Cancel. Allow the Instant Pot to release its pressure naturally for 5 minutes. Using an oven mitt, open the steam-release valve. If there is any steam left over, allow it to release until the silver dial drops, then carefully open the lid.

Serve the bok choy immediately.

CARAMELIZED FENNEL AND TURNIPS

PREP TIME: 20 MINUTES
COOK TIME: 12 MINUTES
TOTAL TIME: 32 MINUTES
YIELD: 4 SERVINGS

Turnips have a lovely flavor, especially when they're caramelized. We love to pair them with fennel, which adds a slightly sweet licorice-like flavor. This quick side dish is perfect served alongside any of your favorite meals.

3 tbsp (45 g) grass-fed butter or ghee

7 medium turnips, peeled and thickly sliced

1 medium bulb fennel, thickly sliced

4 cloves garlic, finely chopped

1 tsp sea salt

1 tsp fresh thyme leaves

½ cup (120 ml) chicken or vegetable broth

1 tbsp (5 g) fresh Italian parsley, finely chopped

Add the butter to the Instant Pot and press Sauté. Once the butter has melted, add the turnips and fennel and sauté for 7 minutes, stirring occasionally, until the vegetables are lightly caramelized. Add the garlic, salt and thyme and sauté for 1 minute, stirring occasionally. Press the Keep Warm/Cancel button.

Add the chicken broth to the Instant Pot.

Place the lid on the Instant Pot, making sure the steam-release valve is sealed. Press the Manual button, and set the Instant Pot for 4 minutes.

When the Instant Pot beeps, press Keep Warm/Cancel. Using an oven mitt, "quick release" the steam-release valve. When the steam stops venting and the silver dial drops, carefully open the lid.

Add the parsley and gently stir until incorporated.

Serve the fennel and turnips immediately.

HEALTHIER SZECHUAN EGGPLANT

PREP TIME: **20 MINUTES**
COOK TIME: **10 MINUTES**
TOTAL TIME: **30 MINUTES**
YIELD: **4 SERVINGS**

Get ready for this eggplant with a mildly spicy kick! My husband is the eggplant guru in our house—his eggplant dishes always turn out perfectly. One of our favorite ways to jazz up eggplant is giving it a little spice and some Asian flavors. By using the Instant Pot's Sauté feature, you lock in the caramelized flavor of the garlicky-ginger eggplant and finish by cooking the eggplant for 2 minutes. It's such an easy, flavorful dish.

3 tbsp (45 g) grass-fed butter or ghee

1½ lb (680 g) Chinese eggplant, cut lengthwise, thickly sliced

4 cloves garlic, finely chopped

2 tbsp (10 g) finely chopped scallions (white and light green parts only)

1 (½-inch [13-mm]) piece fresh ginger, peeled and minced or grated

1½ tbsp (23 ml) coconut aminos or liquid aminos

2 tsp (10 ml) toasted sesame oil

1 tsp granulated erythritol

¾ tsp red pepper flakes

1 tsp sea salt

½ cup (120 ml) chicken or vegetable broth

Add the butter to the Instant Pot and press Sauté. Once the butter has melted, add the eggplant and sauté for 7 minutes, stirring occasionally, until lightly caramelized. Add the garlic, scallions and ginger and sauté for 1 minute, stirring occasionally. Press Keep Warm/Cancel.

Add the aminos, toasted sesame oil, erythritol, red pepper flakes, salt and chicken broth to the Instant Pot.

Place the lid on the Instant Pot, making sure the steam-release valve is sealed. Press the Manual button, and set the Instant Pot for 2 minutes.

When the Instant Pot beeps, press Keep Warm/Cancel. Using an oven mitt, "quick release" the steam-release valve. When the steam stops venting and the silver dial drops, carefully open the lid.

Serve the eggplant immediately.

NOTE: Any variety of eggplant can be used in this dish, such as the common globe eggplant—just chop it into thick pieces.

ZUCCHINI AND SUMMER SQUASH SAUTÉ

PREP TIME: **15 MINUTES**
COOK TIME: **1 MINUTE**
TOTAL TIME: **16 MINUTES**
YIELD: **6 TO 8 SERVINGS**

Zucchini and summer squash are hands down the most-used veggies in our home during the summertime. We make this delicious and easy sauté at least once a week. It also makes its rounds as a side dish to many of our meals.

4 tbsp (60 g) grass-fed butter or ghee or (60 ml) avocado oil

5 medium zucchini, thickly sliced

5 medium summer squash, thickly sliced

1 tsp sea salt

1 tsp granulated garlic or garlic powder

¾ cup (180 ml) chicken broth or vegetable stock

Combine the butter, zucchini, summer squash, salt, granulated garlic and chicken broth in the Instant Pot, stirring a few times. Place the lid on the Instant Pot, making sure the steam-release valve is sealed. Press the Adjust setting until the red light switches to Low Pressure, then press the Manual button and set the Instant Pot for 1 minute.

When the Instant Pot beeps, press Keep Warm/Cancel. Using an oven mitt, "quick release" the steam-release valve. When the steam stops venting and the silver dial drops, carefully open the lid.

Serve the zucchini and summer squash immediately.

NOTE: If you enjoy herby flavors, add ½ teaspoon of one or more of the following dried or fresh herbs: Italian parsley, thyme or dill.

CHEESY GARLIC-HERB SPAGHETTI SQUASH

PREP TIME: **20 MINUTES**
COOK TIME: **10 MINUTES**
TOTAL TIME: **30 MINUTES**
YIELD: **4 SERVINGS**

The Instant Pot is an awesome way to cook spaghetti squash! It steams it so fast and makes it perfectly tender. When cut widthwise, you can get longer strands of squash, making it more like spaghetti—these long squash strands get mixed with garlic, cheese and herbs to create a comforting side dish.

1 medium spaghetti squash

1 cup (240 ml) filtered water

4 tbsp (60 g) grass-fed butter or ghee

5 cloves garlic, minced

2 tsp (2 g) fresh thyme leaves

¼ cup (15 g) finely chopped fresh Italian parsley

¼ cup (12 g) fresh basil, thinly sliced

Zest of 1 lemon

1 tsp sea salt

¼ cup (60 ml) heavy cream

½ cup (50 g) shredded Parmesan cheese

¼ cup (28 g) shredded mozzarella cheese

¼ cup (28 g) shredded provolone cheese

Wash the outside of the squash and use a sharp knife to cut the squash in half widthwise. Use a spoon to scrape out and discard the seeds and stringy parts.

Add the water to the Instant Pot. Place the trivet or a steamer insert inside the pot and place the cut squash on top of the trivet.

Place the lid on the Instant Pot, making sure the steam-release valve is sealed. Press the Manual button, and set the Instant Pot for 8 minutes.

When the Instant Pot beeps, press Keep Warm/Cancel. Using an oven mitt, "quick release" the steam-release valve. When the steam stops venting and the silver dial drops, carefully open the lid.

Carefully remove the squash with tongs and place it on a plate or cutting board. Use a fork to remove the strands of spaghetti squash. Set them aside.

Pour out the water that remains in the pot and return the pot to the Instant Pot. Add the butter to the Instant Pot and press Sauté. Once the butter has melted, add the garlic and thyme and sauté for 2 minutes, stirring occasionally. Add the cooked spaghetti squash, parsley, basil, lemon zest, salt, heavy cream, Parmesan cheese, mozzarella cheese and provolone cheese. Gently toss until everything is combined. Press Keep Warm/Cancel.

Serve the spaghetti squash immediately.

NOTE: You can cut the squash lengthwise, but I prefer to cut it widthwise because you will get longer strands of "spaghetti" compared to the shorter strands you get when you cut the squash lengthwise.

CARAMELIZED HERBY MUSHROOMS

PREP TIME: 20 MINUTES
COOK TIME: 11 MINUTES
TOTAL TIME: 31 MINUTES
YIELD: 4 SERVINGS

These mouthwateringly caramelized mushrooms are so tasty! This classic side dish is well-seasoned with lots of flavor from the golden-brown mushrooms, nutty garlic, dry white wine, tangy lemon and vibrant fresh herbs.

4 tbsp (60 g) grass-fed butter or ghee

2½ lb (1.1 kg) mushrooms, cleaned and halved

4 cloves garlic, finely chopped

½ cup (120 ml) dry white wine

2 tsp (2 g) fresh thyme leaves

1 tsp sea salt

Zest of 1 lemon

2 tbsp (30 ml) fresh lemon juice

¼ cup (15 g) finely chopped fresh Italian parsley

Add the butter to the Instant Pot and press Sauté. Once the butter has melted, add the mushrooms and sauté for 7 minutes, stirring occasionally, until caramelized. Add the garlic and sauté for 1 minute, stirring occasionally. Add the white wine, scraping up any browned bits from the bottom of the pot with a wooden spoon. Press Keep Warm/Cancel.

Add the thyme, salt, lemon zest and lemon juice to the Instant Pot.

Place the lid on the Instant Pot, making sure the steam-release valve is sealed. Press the Manual button, and set the Instant Pot for 3 minutes.

When the Instant Pot beeps, press Keep Warm/Cancel. Using an oven mitt, "quick release" the steam-release valve. When the steam stops venting and the silver dial drops, carefully open the lid.

Add the parsley and stir.

Serve the mushrooms immediately.

NOTE: Freshly grated Parmesan is also delicious as a garnish on top of the mushrooms.

SIMPLE SEA SALT AND HERB SHISHITO PEPPERS

PREP TIME: **15 MINUTES**
COOK TIME: **5 MINUTES**
TOTAL TIME: **20 MINUTES**
YIELD: **4 SERVINGS**

Shishito peppers have become super popular! They're traditionally a part of Asian cuisine, but today they're commonly served as tapas in Spanish restaurants. These perfectly cooked shishito peppers are dressed with melted thyme butter, a nice squeeze of fresh lemon juice and a generous amount of flaked sea salt.

1 cup (240 ml) filtered water

1 lb (454 g) shishito peppers

3 tbsp (45 g) grass-fed butter or ghee

2 tsp (2 g) fresh thyme leaves

1½ tsp (8 g) flaked sea salt

Lemon wedges, as needed

Add the water to the Instant Pot. Place the steamer insert inside the pot and place the shishito peppers on top of the steamer insert.

Place the lid on the Instant Pot, making sure the steam-release valve is sealed. Press the Manual button, and set the Instant Pot for 1 minute.

When the Instant Pot beeps, press Keep Warm/Cancel. Using an oven mitt, "quick release" the steam-release valve. When the steam stops venting and the silver dial drops, carefully open the lid.

Carefully remove the shishito peppers and steamer insert, setting the shishito peppers aside. Pour out the water that remains in the pot and return it to the Instant Pot. Add the butter to the Instant Pot and press Sauté. Once the butter has melted, add the thyme and sauté for 1 minute, stirring occasionally. Add the shishito peppers, sautéing until they start to turn golden brown in some spots, about 3 minutes. Press Keep Warm/Cancel.

Serve the shishito peppers immediately, sprinkled with flaked sea salt and with the lemon wedges on the side.

NOTES: Freshly grated Parmesan is also delicious on top of the cooked shishito peppers. Add the Parmesan at the same time you add the flaked sea salt.

If you prefer, you can skip the sautéing process and place the herb-butter shishito peppers on a medium baking sheet and place it under a preheated broiler for 1 minute, just until the peppers are slightly blistered with a few golden-brown spots.

NO-SUGAR RHUBARB COMPOTE

PREP TIME: 20 MINUTES
COOK TIME: 5 MINUTES
TOTAL TIME: 25 MINUTES
YIELD: 3½ CUPS (840 ML)

The texture and flavor of this simple rhubarb compote is pure perfection. If you're like me, you look forward to the abundance of rhubarb each spring, and this compote is one of my favorite things to cook during this vegetable's short season. It's ready in minutes in the Instant Pot and goes perfectly with savory and sweet dishes.

7 cups (854 g) thickly sliced rhubarb

2 tbsp (30 g) grass-fed butter, ghee or refined coconut oil

¼ tsp sea salt

½ cup (120 ml) filtered water

⅓ cup (40 g) powdered erythritol

Cut off the ends of the rhubarb stalks and discard, then cut the stalks into thick 1-inch (2.5-cm) slices.

Combine the rhubarb, butter, salt and water in the Instant Pot. Place the lid on the Instant Pot, making sure the steam-release valve is sealed. Press the Manual button, and set the Instant Pot for 5 minutes.

When the Instant Pot beeps, press Keep Warm/Cancel. Allow the Instant Pot to release its pressure naturally for 10 minutes. Using an oven mitt, open the steam-release valve. If there is any steam left over, allow it to release until the silver dial drops, then carefully open the lid.

Carefully transfer the cooked rhubarb mixture to a blender or food processor. If there is a lot of excess liquid left over in the pot, only use about half of the liquid. Add the erythritol and pulse just until the mixture is fully combined and smooth, about 30 seconds. You may need to do this in batches if you're using a blender—make sure to leave at least a few inches of space in the blender and not fill it to the top as the hot steam will need room to escape.

Serve the compote warm or cold as a condiment for savory meals or enjoy by the spoonful.

NOTE: Rhubarb is especially delicious paired with poultry like the Citrus-Herb Game Hen (page 65) or fish dishes like the High-Fat Herb-Butter Salmon (page 38) and Halibut with Sweet Strawberry Compote (page 41). It's also delicious paired with desserts.

SWEET INDULGENCES WITHOUT THE GUILT

Who knew that making treats in the Instant Pot could be so much fun and save time too?

Instant Pot desserts often can be made in less than half the time that it would take to bake something in the oven or cook it on the stove. Another plus is that the Instant Pot doesn't heat up your house, which makes it especially great for summertime baking.

You can even bring your Instant Pot on road trips or family functions and make easy, special desserts in your hotel room or on the spot, like Magical Double-Chocolate Brownies (page 172) or Luscious Chocolate Custard (page 164).

What better way to finish an entire meal of Instant Pot–cooked foods than with a decadent treat from your little round "baking" machine. Indulge your sweet tooth with the delectable low-carb, sugar-free desserts in this chapter like Vibrant Lemon Bundt Cake (page 163) and Low-Carb Sour Cream Coffee Cake (page 175).

VIBRANT LEMON BUNDT CAKE

PREP TIME: 25 MINUTES
COOK TIME: 40 MINUTES
TOTAL TIME: 65 MINUTES
YIELD: 8 TO 10 SERVINGS

Lemon desserts make me think of my mom. She made the best lemon squares, and we loved getting slices of iced lemon Bundt cake at her favorite local café. This delicious cake, which is full of lemon zest and fresh lemon juice, reminds me of the lemon desserts we enjoyed together.

¼ cup (60 g) grass-fed butter or ghee, melted and cooled, plus more butter as needed to grease pan

½ cup (60 g) powdered erythritol

¼ cup (60 g) cream cheese, softened

2 large eggs, at room temperature

¼ cup (58 g) sour cream

Zest of 3 lemons

3 tbsp (45 ml) fresh lemon juice

2 tsp (10 ml) pure vanilla extract

½ tsp baking soda

¼ tsp sea salt

1½ cups (144 g) superfine blanched almond flour

1½ cups (360 ml) filtered water

With the extra butter, generously grease a 6- or 7-inch (13- or 15-cm) springform pan, 1½-quart (1.5-L) baking dish or Bundt cake pan that fits in the Instant Pot. If using a baking dish, add a circular piece of unbleached parchment paper that will fit on the bottom of the baking dish. Set aside.

In a large bowl, combine the erythritol and cream cheese. Mix them together with a handheld mixer. Add the eggs, sour cream and ¼ cup (60 g) of butter and mix on low speed, just until combined. Add the lemon zest, lemon juice, vanilla, baking soda, salt and almond flour and mix on low speed, just until incorporated. Do not overmix. Pour the cake batter into the prepared pan.

Place the Instant Pot trivet in the Instant Pot. Pour the water into the Instant Pot. Gently place the pan in the Instant Pot and cover it with a glass baking dish lid. Place the lid on the Instant Pot, making sure the steam-release valve is sealed. Press the Manual button, and set the Instant Pot for 40 minutes.

When the Instant Pot beeps, press Keep Warm/Cancel. Allow the Instant Pot to naturally release its pressure for 15 minutes. Using an oven mitt, "quick release" the steam-release valve. When the steam stops venting and the silver dial drops, carefully open the lid.

Using oven mitts, remove the lid and carefully lift the trivet and the pan out of the Instant Pot. Test the cake for doneness with a toothpick—it should come out with no more than a few moist crumbs. If it's not done, cover and cook for another 3 minutes, then "quick release" the pressure. Allow the cake to cool on a wire rack for 30 minutes. Once it has cooled, gently run a knife around the edges of the cake to loosen it from the pan. Carefully remove it from the pan and allow it to finish cooling on a wire rack. If using a baking dish, invert the cake on a larger serving dish to remove the cake from the dish.

Slice and serve the cake immediately.

NOTES: If you don't have a glass lid, you can cover the top of the pan or dish with unbleached parchment paper, then top it with foil and secure it around the edges.

For an extra special treat, frost the cake with sugar-free, low-carb lemon cream cheese frosting or dust the top with powdered erythritol.

LUSCIOUS CHOCOLATE CUSTARD

PREP TIME: 20 MINUTES
COOK TIME: 5 MINUTES
INACTIVE TIME: 6 HOURS
TOTAL TIME: 6 HOURS, 25 MINUTES
YIELD: 5 SERVINGS

Enjoying homemade custard by the spoonful is so much fun, and this chocolaty goodness is perfect for an afternoon snack or a special treat. This custard reminds me of the chocolate pudding and custard that my grandma would make for me as a young kid— except this version is so much healthier and cooks so much faster!

1½ cups (360 ml) heavy cream

½ cup (120 ml) milk

¾ cup (135 g) finely chopped sugar-free, stevia-sweetened chocolate or chocolate chips

2 large eggs

½ cup (60 g) powdered erythritol

1 tbsp (7 g) cocoa powder

1 tbsp (15 ml) pure vanilla extract

1 tbsp (15 g) grass-fed butter, melted

1 tsp grass-fed bovine gelatin

1 cup (240 ml) filtered water

In a small pot over low heat, warm the cream, milk and chocolate, whisking until the chocolate is melted. Remove the pot from the heat and set aside.

Combine the eggs, erythritol, cocoa powder, vanilla and butter in a blender. Blend on low speed for 30 seconds, until the ingredients are fully combined. While the blender is still running, remove the vent lid and add the chocolate mixture and gelatin and continue to blend for 30 seconds, until fully combined.

Evenly distribute the custard mixture between five 8-oz (240-ml) glass jars, leaving at least ½ inch (13 mm) of space at the top. Cover the jars with lids.

Add the water to the Instant Pot and place the Instant Pot trivet inside the pot. Set all five jars inside the Instant Pot on top of the trivet. They should fit perfectly inside the Instant Pot. Place the lid on the Instant Pot, making sure the steam-release valve is sealed. Press the Manual button, then choose Low Pressure and set the Instant Pot for 5 minutes.

When the Instant Pot beeps, press Keep Warm/Cancel. Using an oven mitt, "quick release" the steam-release valve. When the steam stops venting and the silver dial drops, carefully open the lid.

Using an oven mitt or tongs, carefully remove the jars from the Instant Pot and remove the lids. Stir the custards until the mixture becomes smooth, then allow them to cool at room temperature. Once they have cooled, transfer them to the refrigerator to set. Let them chill for a minimum of 6 hours (preferably overnight for the best texture).

NOTES: Sustainably sourced grass-fed bovine gelatin is sold at most natural-foods stores and is widely available online.

Garnish the custards with homemade whipped cream or coconut whipped cream and shaved sugar-free chocolate.

I use 8-ounce (240-ml) Mason jars with lids for this recipe.

SUGAR-FREE RASPBERRY CHEESECAKE

PREP TIME: **30 MINUTES**
COOK TIME: **57 MINUTES**
INACTIVE TIME: **6 HOURS, 30 MINUTES**
TOTAL TIME: **7 HOURS, 57 MINUTES**
YIELD: **8 TO 10 SERVINGS**

Because of all the baking steps, I'd never been a fan of making cheesecakes, but the Instant Pot changed that. It cooks cheesecake perfectly without a lot of fuss. This raspberry cheesecake is so delicious and full of that classic, creamy cheesecake flavor plus just a hint of sweet berries.

CRUST

2 tbsp (30 g) grass-fed butter or ghee, melted, plus more butter as needed

2 tbsp (32 g) granulated erythritol

1 cup (96 g) superfine blanched almond flour

CHEESECAKE

16 oz (448 g) cream cheese, softened

¼ cup (58 g) sour cream

2 large eggs, at room temperature

¾ cup (90 g) powdered erythritol

¼ cup (80 g) sugar-free, all-fruit, seedless raspberry jam or preserves

1 tsp pure vanilla extract

½ tsp sea salt

1 cup (240 ml) filtered water

RASPBERRY COULIS (OPTIONAL)

8 oz (224 g) fresh or frozen raspberries

1 tbsp (16 g) granulated erythritol

½ tsp grass-fed bovine gelatin

With the extra butter, grease a 6- or 7-inch (15- or 18-cm) springform pan that fits in the Instant Pot. Set aside.

To make the crust, combine the butter, erythritol and almond flour in a medium bowl. Mix the ingredients with your hands until they are completely combined. Transfer the crust mixture to the prepared springform pan and press down to form a packed crust at the bottom. Don't allow too much of the crust to go up the sides of the pan. Transfer the pan to the freezer for 15 minutes.

To make the cheesecake, combine the cream cheese, sour cream, eggs, powdered erythritol, raspberry jam, vanilla and salt in a blender. Blend on low speed until the mixture is smooth and fully combined. Pour the cheesecake filling into the frozen springform pan.

Place the Instant Pot trivet in the Instant Pot. Pour the water into the Instant Pot. Gently place the springform pan in the Instant Pot and cover the pan with a glass baking dish lid. Place the lid on the Instant Pot, making sure the steam-release valve is sealed. Press the Manual button, and set the Instant Pot for 45 minutes.

When the Instant Pot beeps, press Keep Warm/Cancel. Allow the Instant Pot to release its pressure naturally for 15 minutes. Using an oven mitt, "quick release" the steam-release valve. When the steam stops venting and the silver dial drops, carefully open the lid.

Carefully remove the lid and lift the trivet and the cheesecake out of the Instant Pot. Allow the cheesecake to cool to room temperature with the lid still on. Once it has cooled, remove the lid, taking care not to drip any of the condensation on the cheesecake. Gently run a knife around the edges of the cheesecake to loosen it from the sides of the pan. Wipe off all the condensation from the lid and place it back on top of the cheesecake. Transfer the cheesecake to the refrigerator for at least 6 hours (preferably overnight), until completely chilled.

To make the raspberry coulis, place the raspberries and erythritol in a small pot over medium heat and cook for about 10 minutes, stirring occasionally, just until the raspberries break down and become a thick sauce. Sprinkle the gelatin over the top of the sauce and stir until the gelatin has dissolved, about 2 minutes. Pour the sauce into a heatproof bowl and chill it in the refrigerator for 30 minutes. Pour the coulis over the top of the chilled cheesecake.

"JUST LIKE THE REAL DEAL" CHOCOLATE CAKE

PREP TIME: 25 MINUTES
COOK TIME: 25 MINUTES
TOTAL TIME: 50 MINUTES
YIELD: 8 TO 10 SERVINGS

Chocolate cake has always been a favorite of mine. I am definitely the chocolate lover in our family, and I will happily enjoy a slice of frosted chocolate cake any day. The Instant Pot helps lock in the moisture and keep this cake nice and tender. And it tastes scrumptious too!

½ cup (115 g) grass-fed butter or ghee, melted and cooled, plus more butter as needed to grease pan

¾ cup (90 g) powdered erythritol

2 large eggs, at room temperature

½ cup (120 ml) heavy cream

¼ cup (28 g) cocoa powder

½ tsp baking soda

¼ tsp sea salt

2 tsp (10 ml) pure vanilla extract

1 cup (96 g) superfine blanched almond flour

1 cup (240 ml) filtered water

With the extra butter, generously grease a 6- or 7-inch (15- or 18-cm) springform pan or a 1½-quart (1.5-L) baking dish that fits in the Instant Pot. If using a baking dish, add a circular piece of unbleached parchment paper that will fit on the bottom of the baking dish. Set aside.

In a large bowl, combine the butter and powdered erythritol and use a handheld mixer to mix them together. Add the eggs and mix on low speed, just until combined. Add the heavy cream, cocoa powder, baking soda, salt, vanilla and almond flour, mixing by hand with a spatula just until the ingredients are incorporated. Do not overmix. Pour the cake batter into the prepared pan.

Place the Instant Pot trivet in the Instant Pot. Pour the water into the Instant Pot. Gently place the pan in the Instant Pot and cover it with a glass baking dish lid. Place the lid on the Instant Pot, making sure the steam-release valve is sealed. Press the Manual button, and set the Instant Pot for 25 minutes.

When the Instant Pot beeps, press Keep Warm/Cancel. Allow the Instant Pot to release its pressure naturally for 15 minutes. Using an oven mitt, "quick release" the steam-release valve. When the steam stops venting and the silver dial drops, carefully open the lid. Remove the lid and carefully lift the trivet and the pan out of the Instant Pot. Test the cake for doneness with a toothpick—it should come out with no more than a few moist crumbs. If it's not done, cover the pan and cook for another 3 minutes, then "quick release" the pressure.

Allow the cake to cool on a wire rack for 30 minutes. Once it has cooled, gently run a knife around the edges of the cake to loosen it from the pan. Remove it from the pan and allow it to finish cooling on a wire rack. If using a baking dish, invert the cake on a larger serving plate to remove the cake from the dish.

Slice and serve the cake immediately.

NOTE: For an extra special treat, frost the cake with sugar-free, low-carb chocolate buttercream frosting or serve à la mode with a scoop of homemade sugar-free vanilla ice cream.

FLOURLESS STRAWBERRY-RHUBARB CRUMBLE

PREP TIME: 25 MINUTES
COOK TIME: 10 MINUTES
TOTAL TIME: 35 MINUTES
YIELD: 8 SERVINGS

This seasonal crumble has only seven ingredients and takes only ten minutes to cook in the Instant Pot. You can't beat that! It's extra special served à la mode with your favorite sugar-free vanilla ice cream.

CRUMBLE TOPPING

½ cup (48 g) superfine blanched almond flour

½ cup (100 g) granulated erythritol

¼ cup (60 g) cold grass-fed butter or ghee

¼ tsp almond extract

FRUIT FILLING

3 cups (366 g) thickly sliced rhubarb

2 cups (288 g) fresh strawberries, hulled and halved

2 tbsp (15 g) powdered erythritol

1 tsp grass-fed bovine gelatin

1 cup (240 ml) filtered water

To make the crumble topping, in a large bowl, combine the almond flour, granulated erythritol, butter and almond extract, using clean hands to combine the mixture until the cold butter has mixed into the flour and sweetener and it becomes grainy in texture, about 30 seconds. Set aside.

To make the fruit filling, in another large bowl, combine the rhubarb, strawberries, powdered erythritol and gelatin and stir until everything is combined. Set aside.

Add the water to the Instant Pot. Place the steamer trivet inside of the pot with the handles up.

Pour the fruit filling into a round 1½-quart (1.5-L) baking dish with a glass lid or a 6- or 7-cup (1.4- or 1.7-L) round glass dish that fits in the Instant Pot. Place the crumble topping on top of the fruit filling, making sure it covers the entire surface. Cover the baking dish with the glass lid. Place the covered baking dish on top of the steamer trivet. Place the lid on the Instant Pot, making sure the steam-release valve is sealed. Press the Manual button, and set the Instant Pot for 10 minutes.

When the Instant Pot beeps, press Keep Warm/Cancel. Allow the Instant Pot to release its pressure naturally for 15 minutes. Using an oven mitt, "quick release" the steam-release valve. When the steam stops venting and the silver dial drops, carefully open the lid.

Using oven mitts, remove the lid and carefully remove the baking dish from the Instant Pot and place it on a cooling rack. Allow it to cool for at least 20 minutes before serving. If a crispier topping is desired, place the crumble under a preheated broiler for 1 to 2 minutes, just until the top browns slightly, then allow the crumble to cool for 15 minutes before serving.

NOTES: Sustainably sourced grass-fed bovine gelatin is sold at most natural-foods stores and is widely available online.

If you don't have a lid for your baking dish, you can place a piece of parchment paper over the top of the crumble, then cover and secure it with foil.

MAGICAL DOUBLE-CHOCOLATE BROWNIES

PREP TIME: **25 MINUTES**
COOK TIME: **50 MINUTES**
TOTAL TIME: **75 MINUTES**
YIELD: **8 TO 10 SERVINGS**

Who doesn't love brownies? Most of us grew up eating the kind you make from a box, but that's a thing of the past. Made-from-scratch brownies are so good, and you can make them in the Instant Pot.

½ cup (115 g) grass-fed butter or ghee, softened, plus more butter as needed to grease the pan

1 cup (120 g) powdered erythritol

2 large eggs, at room temperature

⅓ cup (37 g) cocoa powder

¼ tsp sea salt

1 tsp pure vanilla extract

¾ cup (72 g) superfine blanched almond flour

¼ cup (45 g) sugar-free, stevia-sweetened chocolate chips

1 cup (240 ml) filtered water

Flaked sea salt, as needed (optional)

With the extra butter, grease a 1½-quart (1.5-L) baking dish with a glass lid that fits in the Instant Pot. Set aside.

In a large mixing bowl, combine the butter and erythritol and use a handheld mixer to mix until the ingredients are soft and fluffy. Add the eggs and mix on low speed, just until combined. Add the cocoa powder, salt, vanilla and almond flour, mixing by hand with a spatula just until the ingredients are incorporated. Do not overmix. Gently fold the chocolate chips into the batter. Pour the batter into the prepared baking dish and cover the dish with its lid.

Place the Instant Pot trivet in the Instant Pot. Pour the water into the Instant Pot. Gently place the covered baking dish in the Instant Pot. Place the lid on the Instant Pot, making sure the steam-release valve is sealed. Press the Manual button, and set the Instant Pot for 50 minutes.

When the Instant Pot beeps, press Keep Warm/Cancel. Allow the Instant Pot to release its pressure naturally for 10 minutes. Using an oven mitt, "quick release" the steam-release valve. When the steam stops venting and the silver dial drops, carefully open the lid.

Remove the glass lid from the baking dish, taking care not to drip any of the condensation on the brownies. Using oven mitts, carefully lift the trivet and the dish out of the Instant Pot. Allow the brownies to cool completely at room temperature.

Once the brownies have cooled, gently run a knife around the edges of the baking dish to loosen the brownies from the dish. Slice and serve the brownies immediately, garnished with the flaked sea salt if desired.

NOTES: If you don't have a glass lid, you can cover the top of the baking dish with unbleached parchment paper, then top it with foil and secure it around the edges.

These brownies are extra special served à la mode with a scoop of homemade sugar-free vanilla ice cream.

LOW-CARB SOUR CREAM COFFEE CAKE

PREP TIME: 25 MINUTES
COOK TIME: 50 MINUTES
TOTAL TIME: 75 MINUTES
YIELD: 8 TO 10 SERVINGS

You don't have to miss out on delectable sour cream coffee cake if you're eating low-carb. This classic brunch food cooks well in the Instant Pot, which locks in the soft texture that everyone loves.

COFFEE CAKE

2 cups (192 g) superfine blanched almond flour

¾ cup (90 g) powdered erythritol

½ tsp baking soda

1 tsp ground cinnamon

½ tsp sea salt

¼ cup (60 g) grass-fed butter or ghee, melted and cooled, plus more butter as needed to grease pan

2 large eggs, at room temperature

1 cup (230 g) sour cream

2 tsp (10 ml) pure vanilla extract

1½ cups (360 ml) filtered water

TOPPING

1 cup (96 g) superfine blanched almond flour

¾ cup (150 g) granulated erythritol

1 tsp ground cinnamon

¼ cup (60 g) grass-fed butter or ghee, melted

With the extra butter, generously grease a 6- or 7-inch (15- or 18-cm) springform pan or a 1½-quart (1.5-L) baking dish or Bundt cake pan that fits in the Instant Pot. If using a baking dish, add a circular piece of unbleached parchment paper that will fit on the bottom of the baking dish. Set aside.

To make the coffee cake, in a large bowl, combine the almond flour, powdered erythritol, baking soda, cinnamon and salt, stirring to mix the ingredients together. Add the butter, eggs, sour cream and vanilla and mix on low speed with a handheld mixer just until the ingredients are combined. Pour half of the batter into the prepared pan. Set the remaining batter aside.

To make the topping, in a medium bowl, combine the almond flour, granulated erythritol, cinnamon and butter. Mix until the ingredients are fully combined. The mixture will be thick but somewhat damp and soft. Evenly sprinkle one-quarter of this mixture on top of the batter in the pan, reserving the remaining three-quarters. Pour the remaining cake batter over the topping and use a spatula to smooth out the batter's surface if needed. Sprinkle the remaining topping over the top of the batter.

Place the Instant Pot trivet in the Instant Pot. Pour the water into the Instant Pot. Gently place the pan in the Instant Pot and cover it with a glass baking dish lid. Place the lid on the Instant Pot, making sure the steam-release valve is sealed. Press the Manual button, and set the Instant Pot for 50 minutes.

When the Instant Pot beeps, press Keep Warm/Cancel. Allow the Instant Pot to release its pressure naturally for 15 minutes. Using an oven mitt, "quick release" the steam-release valve. When the steam stops venting and the silver dial drops, carefully open the lid.

Using oven mitts, remove the lid and carefully lift the trivet and the pan out of the Instant Pot. Test the cake for doneness with a toothpick—it should come out with no more than a few moist crumbs. If it's not done, cover the pan and cook for another 3 minutes, then "quick release" the pressure.

Allow the cake to cool on a wire rack for at least 30 minutes. Once it has cooled, gently run a knife around the edges of the cake to loosen it from the pan. Carefully remove it from the pan and allow it to finish cooling on a wire rack. If using a baking dish, invert the cake on a larger serving plate to remove the cake from the dish.

Slice and serve the cake immediately.

LOW-CARB KEY LIME CHEESECAKE

PREP TIME: **30 MINUTES**
COOK TIME: **50 MINUTES**
INACTIVE TIME: **6 HOURS**
TOTAL TIME: **7 HOURS, 20 MINUTES**
YIELD: **8 TO 10 SERVINGS**

Key lime desserts have always been a favorite of mine. Key lime pie is one of the best treats, but this key lime cheesecake is even more special. Combine the refreshing flavors of key lime pie with rich cheesecake and you have a winner.

CRUST

2 tbsp (30 g) grass-fed butter or ghee, melted, plus more butter as needed to grease the pan

2 tbsp (32 g) granulated erythritol

1 cup (96 g) superfine blanched almond flour

CHEESECAKE

16 oz (448 g) cream cheese, softened

¼ cup (58 g) sour cream

2 large eggs, at room temperature

¾ cup (90 g) powdered erythritol

2 tbsp (30 ml) fresh key lime juice or lime juice

4 tsp (8 g) key lime or lime zest

1 tsp pure vanilla extract

½ tsp sea salt

1 tsp grass-fed bovine gelatin

1 cup (240 ml) filtered water

Thinly sliced key lime or lime (optional)

With the extra butter, grease a 6- or 7-inch (15- or 18-cm) springform pan that fits in the Instant Pot. Set aside.

To make the crust, in a medium bowl, combine the butter, granulated erythritol and almond flour, mixing the ingredients together with clean hands. Transfer the mixture to the springform pan and press down to form a packed crust at the bottom. Don't allow too much of the crust to go up the sides of the pan. Transfer the pan to the freezer for 15 minutes.

To make the cheesecake, combine the cream cheese, sour cream, eggs, powdered erythritol, key lime juice, key lime zest, vanilla, salt and gelatin in a blender. Blend on low speed until the mixture is smooth and fully combined. Pour the cheesecake filling into the frozen springform pan.

Place the Instant Pot trivet in the Instant Pot. Pour the water into the Instant Pot. Gently place the springform pan in the Instant Pot and cover the pan with a glass baking dish lid. Place the lid on the Instant Pot, making sure the steam-release valve is sealed. Press the Manual button, and set the Instant Pot for 50 minutes.

When the Instant Pot beeps, press Keep Warm/Cancel. Allow the Instant Pot to release its pressure naturally for 15 minutes. Using an oven mitt, "quick release" the steam-release valve. When the steam stops venting and the silver dial drops, carefully open the lid.

Carefullly remove the lid and lift the trivet and the cheesecake out of the Instant Pot. Allow the cheesecake to cool, still covered, to room temperature. Once it has cooled, remove the lid, taking care not to drip any of the condensation on the cheesecake. Gently run a knife around the edges of the cheesecake to loosen it from the pan. Wipe off all condensation from the lid and place it back on top of the cheesecake. Transfer the cheesecake to the refrigerator for at least 6 hours (preferably overnight), until completely chilled.

Serve the cheesecake chilled, garnished with sliced key lime if desired.

NOTE: Sustainably sourced grass-fed bovine gelatin is sold at most natural-foods stores and is widely available online.

MACADAMIA–CHOCOLATE CHIP BLONDIES

PREP TIME: 25 MINUTES
COOK TIME: 35 MINUTES
TOTAL TIME: 60 MINUTES
YIELD: 8 TO 10 SERVINGS

Brownies are good, but have you ever had blondies? With the shape and texture of brownies but with a sweet buttery base instead of chocolate, these bars, studded with macadamia nuts and chocolate chips, are sure to please.

¼ cup (60 g) butter or ghee, softened, plus more butter as needed to grease pan

1 cup (120 g) powdered erythritol

2 large eggs, at room temperature

¼ cup (63 g) almond butter

¼ tsp sea salt

1 tsp pure vanilla extract

¾ cup (72 g) superfine blanched almond flour

½ cup (66 g) macadamia nuts, coarsely chopped

½ cup (90 g) sugar-free, stevia-sweetened chocolate chips

1 cup (240 ml) filtered water

With the extra butter, grease a 1½-quart (1.5-L) baking dish with a glass lid that fits in the Instant Pot. Set aside.

In a large bowl, combine the butter and erythritol. Use a handheld mixer to mix until the ingredients are whipped. Add the eggs and almond butter and mix on low speed, just until combined. Add the salt, vanilla and almond flour, mixing by hand with a spatula just until the ingredients are incorporated. Do not overmix. Gently fold the macadamia nuts and chocolate chips into the batter. Pour the batter into the prepared baking dish. Cover the baking dish with its lid.

Place the Instant Pot trivet in the Instant Pot. Pour the water into the Instant Pot. Gently place the covered baking dish in the Instant Pot. Place the lid on the Instant Pot, making sure the steam-release valve is sealed. Press the Manual button and set the Instant Pot for 35 minutes.

When the Instant Pot beeps, press Keep Warm/Cancel. Allow the Instant Pot to release its pressure naturally for 10 minutes. Using an oven mitt, "quick release" the steam-release valve. When the steam stops venting and the silver dial drops, carefully open the lid.

Using oven mitts, remove the lid from the baking dish, taking care not to drip any of the condensation on the blondies, and carefully lift the trivet and the baking dish out of the Instant Pot. Allow the blondies to cool completely at room temperature.

Once the blondies have cooled, gently run a knife around the edges of the baking dish to loosen the blondies. Slice and serve the blondies immediately.

NOTES: If you don't have a glass lid, you can cover the top of the dish with unbleached parchment paper, then top it with foil and secure it around the edges.

These are extra special served à la mode with a scoop of homemade sugar-free vanilla ice cream or with melted sugar-free, stevia-sweetened chocolate chips drizzled over the top.

CARROT CAKE

PREP TIME: **25 MINUTES**
COOK TIME: **45 MINUTES**
TOTAL TIME: **70 MINUTES**
YIELD: **8 TO 10 SERVINGS**

Carrot cake will always remind me of my mom. When I was a little girl, she would take me to her favorite coffee house and treat me to a slice of carrot cake for breakfast. This grain-free version is so much healthier, so go ahead and enjoy a slice with breakfast if you'd like.

¼ cup (60 g) grass-fed butter or ghee, melted and cooled, plus more butter as needed to grease the pan

½ cup (60 g) powdered erythritol

1 large egg, at room temperature

¼ cup (60 ml) heavy cream

¼ cup (58 g) sour cream

Zest of 1 orange

½ tsp baking soda

2 tsp (6 g) ground cinnamon

½ tsp ground cloves

½ tsp ground allspice

¼ tsp sea salt

1 tsp pure vanilla extract

1 cup (96 g) superfine blanched almond flour

1 cup (110 g) peeled and finely shredded carrots

1½ cups (360 ml) filtered water

With the extra butter, generously grease a 6- or 7-inch (15- or 18-cm) springform pan or a 1½-quart (1.5-L) baking dish that fits in the Instant Pot. If using a baking dish, add a circular piece of unbleached parchment paper that will fit on the bottom of the pan. Set aside.

In a large bowl, combine the butter and erythritol. Use a handheld mixer to mix the ingredients together. Add the egg, cream and sour cream and mix on low speed just until the ingredients are combined. Add the orange zest, baking soda, cinnamon, cloves, allspice, salt, vanilla and almond flour and mix on low speed, just until the ingredients are incorporated. Do not overmix. Fold the carrots into the batter just until incorporated. Pour the cake batter into the prepared pan.

Place the Instant Pot trivet in the Instant Pot. Pour the water into the Instant Pot. Gently place the pan in the Instant Pot and cover it with a glass baking dish lid. Place the lid on the Instant Pot, making sure the steam-release valve is sealed. Press the Manual button, and set the Instant Pot for 45 minutes.

When the Instant Pot beeps, press Keep Warm/Cancel. Allow the Instant Pot to release its pressure naturally for 15 minutes. Using an oven mitt, "quick release" the steam-release valve. When the steam stops venting and the silver dial drops, carefully open the lid.

Using oven mitts, remove the lid and carefully lift the trivet and the pan out of the Instant Pot. Test the cake for doneness with a toothpick—it should come out with no more than a few moist crumbs. If it's not done, cover the pan and cook for another 3 minutes, then "quick release" the pressure.

Allow the cake to cool on a wire rack for 30 minutes. Once it has cooled, gently run a knife around the edges of the cake to loosen it from the pan. Carefully remove it from the pan and allow it to finish cooling on a wire rack. If using a baking dish, invert the cake on a larger serving plate to remove the cake from the dish.

Slice and serve the cake immediately.

NOTES: If you don't have a glass lid, you can cover the top of the pan or dish with unbleached parchment paper, then top it with foil and secure it around the edges.

For an extra special treat, frost the cake with sugar-free, low-carb cream cheese frosting.

ACKNOWLEDGMENTS

My husband, Rudy, and I are so grateful for the opportunity to write another cookbook together. Thank you so much to everyone who has supported us and bought our cookbooks.

To Little Love, Tiny Love and the little ones I've been growing during the entire manuscript and photography process: We love you so much!

To my mom, Martha Criswell (my angel): I know you helped get me through this during the hardest times.

To Jennifer Nitrio (my rock) and Nicole Biegenzahn (my soul sister): Thank you for being my best friends. I love you so much, and I'm so grateful for all of your support and our friendship!

To Nona: Thank you for always being there for us and for your constant, continued support.

Thanks to my amazing midwives, who helped support and encourage me during this process and offered gentle reminders to rest and take care of myself.

To Dad and Joan: Thank you for the supportive words and excitement about the book. Dad, thank you so much for making me a backdrop for my photography—it means a lot to me.

To Page Street Publishing and my editors, Sarah Monroe and Jenna Fagan: Thank you so much for giving us another opportunity to publish.

For my longtime loyal readers: Thank you so much for your continued support!

To everyone who bought and supported my first cookbook and our second cookbook, who sent me kind emails, who shared your photos on social media of the Instant Pot meals you cooked from the cookbooks and who wrote thoughtful and kind reviews of the cookbooks, thank you so much.

ABOUT THE AUTHORS

EMILY SUNWELL-VIDAURRI is a water kefir– and chocolate-loving, holistic-minded wife and mommy. She's the author of the cookbooks *The Art of Great Cooking with Your Instant Pot®* and *Amazing Mexican Favorites with Your Instant Pot®* and is the founder of Recipes to Nourish (www.recipestonourish.com), a gluten-free blog focusing on real food and natural living. Having her daughters changed her life. She became mindful of everything that went into her body and started eating real food, making home-cooked, nourishing meals from scratch and living a more natural life.

After traditional medicine failed to help Emily with migraines, autoimmune disease and more health challenges, she turned to whole foods, mindfulness, gratitude practice, natural remedies, self-care, acupuncture and Chinese medicine for healing and overall wellness.

As a wife and mommy dedicated to making nourishing food and using safe products for her family, she works to empower her readers by showing them that there is a healthier way to eat and live. Her passion is to make healthy, natural living as uncomplicated and enjoyable as possible. She and her family live in Sacramento, California.

RODOLFO "RUDY" VIDAURRI, a former chef and nutritionist, is the coauthor of the cookbook *Amazing Mexican Favorites with Your Instant Pot®*. He is a mixed martial arts trainer who is driven by wellness of the body, mind and soul. It is his mission to inspire and teach the ways of preparing and enjoying real food while instilling the discipline and philosophy of a balanced mind through physical fitness. It is his firm belief that mental stability and wellness is a direct reflection of what we eat.

Rudy is originally from northern California. He taught himself how to cook at the age of sixteen, after his father passed away, because his mother worked long hours. After many trial-and-error recipes, he eventually found that not only was he not messing the food up but also that he was being complimented on it. He soon began to cater dinner parties and worked as a personal chef before he got his professional start at a prominent five-star restaurant in Sacramento, California.

Rudy later attended college in southern California and lived there for more than a decade, working as a chef, musician and fighter. It was there that he discovered his abilities as a cook. He made his way through a range of different restaurants, including some nice ones in the Beverly Hills area and some not-so-nice ones to keep bringing home a paycheck. Through it all he worked his way up to sous chef but didn't realize his true potential until he came back home from Los Angeles and reunited with his high school sweetheart and now wife, Emily, and started his real-food journey. It was with Emily's influence that he changed directions as a cook and realized that great-tasting food could in fact be made with healthier, whole-food ingredients.

Rudy assisted Emily on her first cookbook, *The Art of Great Cooking with Your Instant Pot®*, and now contributes to her esteemed blog, Recipes to Nourish. It is his greatest joy as a cook to make food for his family and see them smile.

INDEX